DATE DUE			
Sep 11'69			
Nov 5 70			
May 23 '72			
Dec 13 '72			
GAYLORD M-2			PRINTED IN U.S.A.

THE GERMAN DRAMA
OF THE
NINETEENTH CENTURY

THE GERMAN DRAMA

OF THE

NINETEENTH CENTURY

BY

Dr. GEORG WITKOWSKI

Professor in the University of Leipzig

AUTHORIZED TRANSLATION
FROM THE SECOND GERMAN EDITION

BY

L. E. HORNING

BENJAMIN BLOM  New York/London

832.009
W 78g
67166
Sept. 1969

First published 1909
Reissued 1968 by Benjamin Blom, Inc.
Bronx, N.Y. 10452

Library of Congress Catalog Card No. 68-20230

Manufactured in the United States of America

PREFACE TO SECOND EDITION

Apart from some small formal changes, this edition differs from the first in that, in deference to many expressed wishes, Romantic opera is treated in a special chapter and that the new works of the dramatists who had become known before 1900 are added as far as they come into consideration from the earlier view-point. On the other hand, the time has not yet come for a description of the whole development after the year 1900.

GEORG WITKOWSKI.

Leipzig, July 4, 1906.

PREFACE TO FIRST GERMAN EDITION

This little book had its origin in University-extension lectures given in Leipzig and Altenburg and is first of all an attempt to pave the way for an understanding of the drama of the present day from an historical standpoint. Therefore the chief weight is laid upon those historical factors which settle the last stages of development, and the three factors of dramatic production, art-view, actor's art and public, are considered side by side in accordance with their importance. The musical drama and the lesser varieties had also to be sketched in their development if the picture was to correspond to reality. True, the outward form and the brief contents forced me just in these points to introduce merely the essential changes of each variety from one period to another and to illustrate them by some characteristic productions. In other respects the work imposed rendered it necessary to limit myself to the *historically* important persons and works. But those names at least should not be lacking for which the reader will look first of all because they are reckoned with those which are mentioned most often in histories of literature or of the stage. That I have also mentioned some dramas which appeared after the year 1900, in order to complete the picture of the dramatists who up to that time had already become important, will not be felt as a violence done to the limit given in the title.

Leipzig, January 3, 1904.

TRANSLATOR'S PREFACE

Professor Witkowski's little book appealed to me from the first as a very sane and suggestive introduction, and when my good fortune took me to Leipzig in 1906 we soon became good friends. The desire to see the work turned into English was mutual and the publishers readily gave their consent.

In only one instance have I made any departure from the text of the second German edition. In this case I have made use of an expression from Prof. Witkowski's last letter to me with the result that the passage seems to me more definite and the meaning clearer.

The dates are those of the original and differ in a few instances from those of other works. I have not the means of settling these differences finally.

The figures in the repertoire lists might have been extended in the English edition to cover the years 1905–06 and 1906–07. But they would have made little difference in the conclusions drawn. They would have shown: that Faust Part II is increasingly played, as one might easily conclude from the fact that at least *three* new stage-versions of Faust have appeared within the last two years; that Laube, Gutzkow and Freytag seem to be more popular; that Halm shows signs of revival; that Schneider's little work suffered a temporary eclipse in 1904–05; that Benedix dies hard; that Hebbel and Anzengruber are rapidly gaining in favor with the public.

To my wife I am under a heavy debt for her close criticisms, her helpful and suggestive advice.

L. E. HORNING.

University of Toronto (Victoria College),
    April, 1909.

CONTENTS.

THE GERMAN DRAMA

OF THE

NINETEENTH CENTURY

GERMAN DRAMA AT THE CLOSE OF THE EIGHTEENTH CENTURY

AT the beginning of the nineteenth century middle-class drama on the German stage far surpassed all other varieties in numbers and popularity. Lessing had laid the foundation for it and made it free from French influence. *Miss Sara Sampson* (1755), *Minna von Barnhelm* (1767) and *Emilia Galotti* (1772) were the earliest prototypes of a realistic art which took its subjects from contemporaneous life and substituted deep feeling in unadorned prose for the unnatural sentiment of the Alexandrine tragedy. In his *Hamburgische Dramaturgio* (1768–69) Lessing showed that the French were wrong in asserting the conformity of their rules with the laws of Aristotle, and pointed to Shakespeare as the greatest tragic poet of modern times.

Contempt for rules, enthusiasm for Shakespeare and a striving for a characteristic national art led to the production, in the "Storm and Stress" period, of a succession of works which lent gifted expression to the feelings and longings of the German youth. At the head of this list was Goethe's first great work, *Götz von Berlichingen* (1773). For the first time the past of their own people lived before them in a genuine historical drama, but it was too disconnected in form and this prevented its becoming popular on the stage. The numerous imitations, none of which approached the *Götz* in poetic merit, succeeded in avoiding this fault

1

and the clang of armor resounded on the German stage far down into the nineteenth century.

The contemporaries of Goethe's youth, Lenz, Klinger and Heinrich Leopold Wagner, did not satisfy the demands of the stage any better than he had done. Accordingly a permanent influence was not exercised by their dramas which, by their treatment of contemporaneous social problems, enlarged the previously narrow horizon of the middle-class drama. In Schiller's early dramas, *Die Räuber* (1781) and *Kabale und Liebe* (1784), these new motives were, for the first time, united by the unerring judgment of a great and born dramatist with what was suited to the stage and with a complete mastery of realistic style. After completing *Don Carlos* (1787) he turned to that idealistic style, characterized by the external form of the verse, which Lessing had already made use of in his dramatic poem *Nathan der Weise* (1779). These two works exerted at first just as little influence on succeeding works as did Shakespeare's dramas, which the great actor, Friedrich Ludwig Schröder, had been playing in Germany since 1776, or Goethe's new and lofty dramas, *Iphigenie auf Tauris* (1787), *Egmont* (1788), *Torquato Tasso* (1790). Like the fragment *Faust,* which appeared at the same time as *Tasso,* they remained entirely unnoticed.

The operetta, for the most part the harmless representation of slightly idealized rural situations, interwoven with simple melodious songs, had taken triumphant possession of the German stage since 1766. It reached its highest development in the operas of MOZART, *Belmont und Constanze* (1782), and *Die Zauberflöte* (1791). At this time middle-class drama received new life from the quickly passing "Storm and Stress" influence. The subjects treated by this class of writers were taken hold of but fashioned according to the temper of timid middle-class ethics: the collisions which led to the catastrophe in the former found a happy solution in the latter. The middle-class saw its own joys and sorrows mirrored in these plays and the great mass of spectators were delighted and moved to tears by the conscientious treatment of the conditions and events of their daily life. What did it matter if commonplace reality was presented without any claims to artistic excellence, if Teutomania, moralizing, effeminate sentimentality, one-sided glorification of the middle classes at the expense of all others, and theatrical convention robbed the portrait of truth and higher merit? BARON OTTO VON GEMMINGEN produced the first example of this class in *Der deutsche Hausvater* (1780) and AUGUST WILHELM IFFLAND, actor and manager in Mannheim and Berlin, cultivated it with the greatest success. His best works, *Die Jäger* (1781), *Die Hagestolzen* (1791), *Der Spieler* (1796) held their place long after the middle of the nineteenth century. Iffland's plays were suited exactly to the taste of the middle-class public. He excluded all great historical events, all political questions and all references to public affairs. The home alone was his world and this he delineated with the care of a miniature painter. In all his plays he shows persecuted virtue finally overcoming vice and from need and poverty attaining to prosperity. An easy comfortable life and the middle-class "Reputation" are with him the most important matters; for their sake ethical blemishes are tolerated wherever they admit of being glossed over. With Iffland guilt is not an offence against universal order, a conflict of the passions with divine and human laws, but merely the crime which falls within the province of the police and the reformatory. Iffland's plays offer actors many acceptable rôles and their after-effect may be traced right down to the present.

In respect to duration and strength of influence only one writer can be compared to Iffland, namely, his somewhat younger contemporary, AUGUSTUS KOTZEBUE. But the same expedients which Iffland employed for an honorable purpose are in Kotzebue degraded to the service of speculation on lower impulses. In his works the frivolous noble is contrasted with the worthy citizen, the Germans are honorable, the foreigners rascals and deceivers. He does not, however, use these contrasts from an honest patriotic conviction but merely to flatter his hearers; they are with him, like everything else, only means to the sole end of external success. Thus his great talent, in spite of the enormous production of over two hundred dramatic works, brought no lasting good to the German stage. Owing to the fact that he everywhere aimed at light superficial entertainment he became for a long time the real ruler of the stage and even in the Weimar theatre when conducted by Goethe no author was played so often as Kotzebue. He tried his hand at all varieties from lofty tragedy to vulgar farce, with the greater success the lower his view-point, and the more he aimed with coarse but sure art at the momentary effect of pealing laughter or of cheap emotion. His favorite characters are those which deviate from the path of virtue: fallen women and girls whose misfortune is deplored and represented as the consequence of excusable human weakness; frivolous seducers transfigured by the splendor of knightly charm; immature, naïvely lascivious girls, the forerunners of the modern *demi-vierges,* and aging worldlings.

Menschenhass und Reue (1787) brought Kotzebue his first and greatest success. It was for a long time the favorite play of the entire German public and was also received in London, Paris and Madrid with an applause such as only Goethe's *Werther* met with among all German writings in foreign lands. A long succession of other very influential works followed, among which possibly *Die Unglücklichen* (1798), *Die beiden Klingsberg* (1801), *Die deutschen Kleinstädter* (1803) and *Pagenstreiche* (1804) may be regarded as having relatively the greatest merit, because in them Kotzebue's talent for the comic of environment and his unerring command of all the devices of technique is best shown.

All those who took German art seriously rightly saw in him its most dangerous enemy. When Schiller, after a long interruption, turned again to dramatic poetry in *Wallenstein* (1800) he had to try and combat the moral weakness of the time which manifested itself in its favorite authors. He wished to unite proportion, harmony, grandeur, intrinsic truth and beautiful form; he substituted an inspired rhythmical, elevated language for prose and for the ethical code of the period of enlightenment, an exalted idealism which was filled with pride in its independence, won by mighty will-power, of all the accidental conditions of existence. Schiller now strove for an effect similar to the overpowering force of Greek tragedy, and sought to unite the lofty dignity of the ancients with the technique of Shakespeare, the demand for moral freedom with the fatalism of classical authors. Each of his dramas from *Wallenstein* onwards represents an attempt to combine these opposing conceptions of life and art: none is entirely successful. The depths of the gulf which he wishes to bridge over is most clearly recognisable in *Wallenstein* and in *Die Braut von Messina* (1803) but even the two intermediate works, *Maria Stuart* (1801) and *Die Jungfrau von Orleans* (1802), as well as his last completed drama, *Wilhelm Tell* (1804), and the powerful fragment *Demetrius* bear witness that the problem is not capable of solution. The lofty sentiment, the tumultuous rhetorical movement, the accurate calculation of effect, and above all the incomparable dramatic instinct of the poet, do not easily allow the disinterested spectator to become conscious of the inherent faults in these great works. Schiller himself clearly recognized them and, when death suddenly carried him off, he was on the way to a realism which derives the fate of man solely from his will and desires. That it was no longer permitted him to give form to this conception in new works, is the greatest misfortune which has happened to German drama. As it was, his last works had to rank for the host of imitators as absolutely classical models and the conviction took root that only in this form was dramatic poetry of lofty style possible.

This error was strengthened and kept alive by the fact that the following period did not produce a German dramatist who, like Schiller, was capable of combining the highest artistic purposes with noble conformity to national character and of gaining in this way a lasting influence over the great masses. His greatest contemporary, Goethe, wrote the stage a farewell letter when he gave to his people the first part of *Faust,* which for all that could not remain a stranger to the stage because its wealth of original poetic power was too great. But when working at the second part, to which he gave form in extreme old age, Goethe had before his eyes a scene of action which was not yet in existence. With unceasing effort the German stage is grappling with this work which one day must become its greatest possession.

GERMAN DRAMA FROM 1800–1830.

ROMANTIC DRAMA

THE predominant literary movement of the first three decades of the nineteenth century was not favorable to the creation of drama. The Romanticists did not give to the stage a single work of lasting importance. The great dramatic writers of this period, Kleist and Grillparzer, went each his own way, the former scarcely heeded, the latter, after the great triumphs of his first works, soon frightened away from the theatre by animosity and lack of appreciation. The field of lofty tragedy belonged to the imitators of Schiller; in play and comedy Iffland and Kotzebue remained the masters and models. Only the dialect play and the romantic opera developed new, independent growth.

Goethe and Schiller have their heroes come into conflict with the objective world-order and go under because they will not renounce their claims, which are subjectively justifiable but objectively unjustifiable. On the other hand the theory of the Romanticists is unlimited subjectivity, their law of life and art is caprice which acknowledges no power above itself. From this follow definite consequences for the form and contents of the creations. There is no definite, clearly recognized goal, no strong clear-cut purpose out of which the action necessarily grows, but instead we have moods, dependence upon outward impressions, sensations, aimless wanderings in life and in the unbounded world of phantasy, delight in what is novel, curious, mysterious or mystical. There is a lack of clear modelling, a striving after picturesque and musical effects, a preference for lyric form, and especially for the prose romance, the loose technique of which seems to give the freest play to caprice.

In this art there is no place for drama. The dramatic works of the Romanticists contradict either their own principles or the nature of the class. We are indebted to them for only one great production, which has been of the greatest service to the German stage and the further evolution of our dramatic writings, viz: the translation of the works of Shakespeare. True, Wieland had already turned most of them into German, with gaps here and there, with many mistakes and without penetrating into the spirit of the author and of his times. It was only when AUGUST WILLIAM SCHLEGEL, in 1797-1801, offered sixteen plays in a masterly version that the greatest dramatist of all time was really won for Germany. Schlegel himself translated afterwards but one additional drama (*Richard III*), the rest were the work of Count Wolf Baudissin and Ludwig Tieck's daughter Dorothea. In 1825–1833 this so-called Schlegel-Tieck Shakespeare appeared and is, in spite of occasional faults, the greatest monument since Luther's Bible to the skill of German translators.

For a time Calderon's plays also exercised a strong influence upon the German drama. These were translated by Aug. W. Schlegel under the title, *Spanisches Theater*. Through them the trochaic tetrameter became popular for plays of romantic character and this form of verse obtained long after the early enthusiasm for Calderon had died out.   In his lectures on *Dramatic Art and Literature* (1808) Schlegel laid the foundation of an historical interpretation which placed modern art on an equality with the classical, Shakespeare and Calderon being the central figures.   This widely known work has become very important as a basis of historical judgment: the main lines of its division are still authoritative to-day.   And yet August William Schlegel did not draw them himself but took them over from his more original brother, Friedrich.   For these reasons the Schlegel brothers really deserved well of the German stage in spite of the fact that as independent authors they each produced but one failure, the dramas *Alarcos* (1802) and *Ion* (1803).

The single writer of the Elder Romantic school who wrote numerous works in dramatic form was LUDWIG TIECK, but he, too, was no dramatist.   Schiller's judgment concerning him gives the explanation: ''His is a very graceful, fanciful, gentle nature, he merely lacks strength and depth and always will.''   In *Der gestiefelte Kater* (1797) the fairy-story serves only as an excuse for ridiculing his opponents, Iffland, Kotzebue and the age of Enlightenment.   As he does not produce a drama, but merely gives the description of the staging of a drama, he disregards completely a compact dramatic form. The same thing happens in another way in the *Leben und Tod der heiligen Genoveva* (1799) and in *Kaiser Octavianus* (1804).   Both are large pictures glorifying the Middle Ages and made up of lyric and epic parts.

Tieck studied the stage closely from his youth up and as editor, translator and critic produced valuable works such as his *Altenglisches Theater* (1811), *Deutsches Theater* (1817) *Shakespeares Vorschule*

(1823–29) and *Kritische Schriften* (1848). However little he followed the laws of dramatic creation in his own writings, he was thoroughly acquainted with them. Germany has had few students of the drama with the same sound judgment.

The gifted CLEMENS BRENTANO was directly inspired by Tieck. His *Gustav Wasa* (1800) imitates to excess *Der gestiefelte Kater*, his historical romantic drama, *Die Gründung Prags* (1815), is just as lacking in form and as insipid as the *Genoveva*. He appears more independent in the clever comedy, *Ponce de Leon* (1804), though it, too, is unsuited to acting, and in the sprightly vaudeville *Die lustigen Musikanten* (1803).

The other dramas in Romantic style by Wilhelm von Schütz, Achim von Arnim, Friedrich de la Motte-Fouqué and Joseph von Eichendorff are equally unimportant for the stage.

Better success attended the Danish author, ADAM GOTTLIEB OEHLENSCHLÄGER, who followed the German Romanticists most closely and spread their views in his own country. He wrote in German and Danish. In his fairy-drama, dedicated to Goethe, *Aladdin oder die Wunderlampe* (1808), he was still noticeably influenced by Tieck, in his highly successful *Correggio* (1816) he wrote the tragedy, often retold afterwards, of the artist who shipwrecks because a contemptible world does not understand him.

The greatest master of form among his contemporaries, ERNST AUGUST, GRAF VON PLATEN-HALLERMÜNDE, showed himself to be an artist in clash with existing reality. His comedy, *Der gläserne Pantoffel* (1823), utilizes the fairy-stories of *Aschenbrödel* and *Dornröschen*, in the same way as Tieck had before used *Der gestiefelte*

Kater, to sketch, by a mixture of forms in Romantic fashion, a picture of society colored by ironic contrasts. Then he turned his attention to comedy in the style of Aristophanes. In this however, he did not, like his classic model, treat the great questions of the time, but only ridiculed, from the view-point of superior intelligence and a high art-ideal, the phenomena of intellectual life which did not appeal to him. Thus in *Schatz des Rhampsinit* (1824) he scourged the Hegelian philosophy, in *Die verhängnissvolle Gabel* (1826) the Fate-tragedy, in *Der Romantische Ödipus* (1829) "the whole mad company of poetasters, which improvises feverish dreams upon the dulcimer and profanes our noble German language." Especially in the addresses to the audience, where the author interrupts the action and speaks to the public himself, he pours out his contempt upon everything which seems to him vulgar or contrary to art. The lofty pathos of tragedy is here united effectively with low, oftentimes very comical pictures and expressions. The figures, however, are not clear, but are representatives of whole schools and only the brilliant cleverness of form could delude one into overlooking the lack of true poetry.

Platen was as powerless to win success on the stage as his opponent, KARL LEBRECHT IMMERMANN, who in *Cardenio und Celinde* (1826), speculating on the delight in the horrible, gave new form to a repulsive subject from Andreas Gryphius which Achim von Arnim had already used. The *Trauerspiel in Tirol* (1828) aimed at presenting in a great historical picture, the fight for independence of the mountain-folk against the French, but Immermann did not know how to portray convincingly either the Alpine world or the simple heart-life of its

inhabitants. And even with the aid of fictitious characters no dramatic action resulted. A revision by the
author under the title *Andreas Hofer* did as little to remove these faults as did later attempts by others down
to the most recent times. Immermann portrayed the
fate of the mightiest of the Hohenstaufens in his tragedy
Kaiser Friedrich II (1828) from the view-point that
the victory of a pure and mighty Catholicism over the
liberal thinker, even the most powerful, represents the
final outcome. He does not aim, like his contemporary
Raupach, at recounting the historic course of events; on
the contrary, a fictitious family-tragedy stands in the
foreground. The same applies also to his trilogy *Alexis*
(1832) in which the contrast between Peter the Great
and his unfortunate son is represented as a similar one
in *Don Carlos.* As author Immermann produced his
best work in the thoughtful dramatic myth *Merlin*
(1832), though with complete disregard of what was
suitable for the stage.

FATE TRAGEDY

Among the Romanticists ZACHARIAS WERNER was the
only one who understood how to unite the tendencies
of the school with a form suitable for acting. His
great importance in the history of the drama does not
depend upon the effective but mystical and emotional
play, *Martin Luther oder die Weihe der Kraft* (1806),
or upon any other of his bulky dramas, but upon a tragedy in one act entitled *Der vierundzwanzigste Februar.*
"Under Goethe's auspices" it was written in 1809 and
was the first of the Fate-tragedies which for some years
dominated the stage. The contradiction between classi-

cal fatalism and the modern world-philosophy, which
Schiller had not been able to overcome, is here adjusted
by the introduction of a wilful, malicious chance plotting
the destruction of men, in the place of a great and
powerful fate. In superstition, in wanton joy in the
horrible and the uncanny lies the cause of the vogue of
the Fate-tragedy which, however, quickly passed. Even
in the individual works of Tieck this trend appeared.
Its origin was favored by Schiller's *Braut von Messina,*
with this difference, that Schiller never degrades to
low designs the fate which obstinately and at all costs
carries through its predetermined purposes; on the contrary he succeeds in getting out of it an effect deeply
thrilling and exalted.

Of this there is no trace in the best of the real Fate-
tragedies, Werner's plays. The spectator receives only
the impression of horror. At the same time *Der vierundzwanzigste Februar* is the work of a poet, while his
imitators try to obtain the same success with ineffective
mechanical construction. The calculating, unsympathetic ADOLPH MÜLLNER, who had before composed comedies in Kotzebue's style, wrote in direct dependence on
Werner, *Der neunundzwanzigste Februar* (1812), also
a tragedy in one act. He heaps up the horrors; bigamy,
incest, childmurder, blizzards at night, solitude, thirst
for blood are made use of to increase the terror as
much as possible, and as an effective addition an effeminate sentimentality is introduced. His success was so
great that Müllner in the very same year wrote a second play of four acts in the same style, *Die Schuld.*
The same ingredients are here mingled just as unpleas-
antly as before, with such accurate calculation that they
deceived not only the mass of the spectators but also

many penetrating critics. By many Werner and Müllner were at the time considered worthy successors of Schiller. No wonder that now a great flood of worthless Fate-tragedies swept over the land, each and all portraying the operations of a secret inevitable power which by preference makes use of certain days and objects for its fateful interference in human destinies, avenges the iniquity of the fathers upon the children and finds rest only when the family, the source of the crime, is exterminated. How strong the influence of the Fate-drama was at that time is clear from the fact that even GRILLPARZER bases his first work, *Die Ahnfrau,* upon fatalistic ideas and that HEINRICH HEINE follows in the footsteps of Werner and Müllner in the only two tragedies he wrote, *Ratcliffe* and *Almansor* (1823), which, in other respects as well, were complete failures.

HEINRICH VON KLEIST

The great writer who, after the death of Schiller, might have been named to continue the evolution of German drama to modern and national form could find no hearing in the age of Romanticism and of Fatedrama. Thanks to the exertions of Ludwig Tieck, public attention began to turn to him in the second decade of the nineteenth century without, however, his being recognized in his true greatness and historical importance. Only much later did it become clear that HEINRICH VON KLEIST, while he was aiming to unite the art of Æschylus and Shakespeare, was on the way to a new and national drama in harmony with the spirit of the age.

Bernd Heinrich Wilhelm von Kleist, born at Frankfort on the Oder, Oct. 18, 1777, became an author late in life. At the age of fifteen, as a member of an old Prussian family of soldiers, he joined the Guards in Potsdam, serving reluctantly. During the Rhine campaign of 1792 he felt the deep gulf between the duties of a man and those of a soldier. In 1799 he gave up his military position but again and again sought refuge under the wings of the Prussian eagle when life pressed him too hard. In his native city he collected with an insatiable thirst literary, historical and philosophical knowledge and thereby probably laid the foundation of that derangement which all too soon was to lame his power of will and purpose. His portrait shows a beardless boyish face with melancholy eyes, lines of suffering about the mouth and a splendid forehead. His intercourse with the cultured circles of Berlin, to which city he returned in 1800, awakened in him the idea of winning bread and fame as an author. He soon found in Robert Guiskard's fate a subject of imposing grandeur. In fruitless wrestling with this task he dissipated his life's energies during the following years. Restlessly he wandered away from his native place. Paris could not give him peace nor was his hope fulfilled that in Switzerland, in the idyllic quiet of country life, he would recover from his unrest. A few months only of happy life were granted him while he led in Berne the modest life of a poet in company with the sons of Wieland and Solomon Gessner and with Heinrich Zschokke. For a time he now allowed his *Robert Guiskard* to drop into the background, and his first work, *Die Familie Schroffenstein,* took form. In spite of the fact that Ludwig Uhland, who looked after its publication, subjected it to a thorough revision, even in this form it still bears testimony to the independent originality of Kleist, scarcely influenced by any predecessors.

Not from the mighty primal impulses of mankind but from distrust, that black poison of the soul, does ruin proceed. It destroys both sexes; the blossoms of love, unfolding amid hate and murder with magical fragrance, fade away under its pestilential breath. With compelling necessity the course of action follows from the given data and the characters are seen to be most sharply and realistically conceived. Most remarkable is the difference between his language and that of his predecessors. In place of the figurative, copious and sentimental diction of Schiller, gilded over with an even brilliancy, in Kleist exuberance and concise brevity appear in turn. His pictures do not disdain the repulsive and common, but every shade of thought and feeling is brought to clearest expression. Acute, indeed subtle explanations are introduced while the action rushes on. Limpid flow is lacking in the verse, oftentimes the sentences burst forth and tumble over each other like rocks down the mountain. Men forge their own fates, there is no interference by a higher power standing apart from the world of reality.

In the second work of these months at Berne, Kleist gave to German literature one of its best comedies, *Der zerbrochene Krug*. The same pleasure in acute argumentation, noticeable in *Die Familie Schroffenstein,* is found in this play. The effective forms of legal proceedings, which writers were very fond of using at the beginnings of German comedy and especially in the carnival-plays, are here taken up again for a higher purpose. For no longer is it a question of the reproduction of an amusing scene; here a human figure of the significance of a type appears in the village magistrate, Adam, who with low, foxy shrewdness tries to turn the suspicion for the deed he himself has done upon another, and thereby becomes involved deeper and deeper in ruin. This court-scene is a really brilliant performance but fitted out with a wealth of striking features almost too great for the stage. It serves, however, the purpose of giving an impression of the most complete material reality. In this regard the play forms a striking contrast to the unpractical idealism of his predecessors and contemporaries.

Lastly, in Switzerland, too, *Robert Guiskard* developed more and more towards completion. But we only possess a few introductory scenes which Kleist restored with difficulty after he had destroyed the great play in a paroxysm of the blackest despair. The fragment takes its place among the greatest dramatic creations of all time. In it the difference between the ancient and the modern view-point is overcome by putting in the place of fate the plague, that inexorable power which rules in the world of reality and which cuts down men without any consideration for their plans and purposes. The style unites the dignified power of Æschylus with the passionate subjectivity of modern writers. The chief characters stand out at the very first glance in plastic beauty and are at the same time endowed with a rich soul-life full of splendor and color. The function of the Greek chorus is represented by individuals taken from the whole body who give expression to the feelings of all.

After he had come through a severe illness in Switzerland, Kleist was justified in venturing with *Robert Guiskard* to try to gain admission into the circle of noble spirits who had come together in Weimar. Wieland especially gave him a kindly welcome, Schiller also made him advances in a friendly spirit and Goethe tried to constrain him to co-operation in his works, though they appealed but little to his nature. But the morbid ambition of Kleist could not submit to looking up to the great man of Weimar. "I will tear the wreath from his brow," he cried, and was consumed with passionate, fruitless incitement of his own powers; "Hell gave me my half-talent, Heaven gives a whole or none at all." He could not endure the serene air of Weimar. Once more he was driven to restless wandering through the world and the end was that destruction of his great life-work, which meant renunciation of all his plans. Modestly he re-entered the Civil service and in Königsberg he found a couple of years of quiet, during which first of all he made his thoughtful recast of the *Amphitryon* legend. No longer, as with Pláutus and Molière who had treated it before him, is the subject ridicule of the deceived husband; it is rather the almost tragic perplexity of feeling on the part of the constant and faithful wife Alkmene. When the god avows to her that he had come to her in the form of her husband, then holy tremors pass over her but she wishes this night blotted out of her memory. There is something allied to the mysteries of the Christian religion in this new, soulful content given to the old heathen legend.

Penthesilea, likewise begun in Königsberg, also lays bare the innermost depths of a woman's heart. Again a new content is given to a Greek legend, which to our modern feeling is scarcely comprehensible. By endowing the heroine with a supreme need for love and at the same time with an unconquerable desire to gain the mastery over her lover, the poet creates an extreme type, a strange mixture of attractive and repulsive features, but after all grand and symmetrical. All the charm of his language, melodious and yet not cloying, of his images full of feeling and picturesque effects, Kleist poured out in the *Penthesilea* as in no other work; and yet it is just the very one which is most difficult to comprehend.

He only finished it in Dresden, after the misfortunes of the Fatherland had startled him out of his brief period of quiet in Königsberg and an unfortunate incident had caused him to be thrust into prison in France. And now for the third time he tried again, from another point of view, to portray the essential character of the loving wife. As a companion picture to *Penthesilea* he wrote *Käthchen von Heilbronn,* whose heroine voluntarily endures every ill treatment and every disgrace which the loved one heaps upon her. Clothed with all the charm of the fairy-story the gracious figure had an effect like a miraculous picture. But in contradistinction to the vague, fantastic manner with which the Romanticists of his day treated similar subjects, here everything is set forth clearly and definitely. Kleist chose the popular form of the drama of chivalry and by a revision met the requirements of the stage better than he had done before. For this reason *Käthchen* attained a popularity beyond any of his other works and was proof even against the wretched stage-versions in which it had to appear.

A burning hatred of Napoleon drove the author out of Dresden when Austria rose in 1809 to fight for freedom. At that time he wrote *Die Hermannsschlacht* to inspire the Germans to a national war against the conqueror. But embittered passion could produce no work of art and the unsuitable material, which had always been intractable to dramatists, helped to bring about the failure of this powerful drama, though it was very impressive in individual passages.

When Austria was vanquished, Kleist again and for the last time sought help in Berlin. He brought with him a new work, *Der Prinz von Homburg,* a companion piece to *Hermannsschlacht.* It showed where the poet saw the hope for the salvation of his native country, namely, in the Prussian spirit of unconditional obedience and in a readiness to sacrifice everything for the state. Kleist does not make his prince despise death like the ordinary heroes of tragedy; on the contrary, he trembles so violently in its presence that everything else in comparison with mere existence seems as nothing. But the conviction of the necessity of discipline conquers even this fear of death and the prince is ready to suffer the punishment he has deserved for his transgression. Thus the power of the sense of duty, through which Prussia has become great, is upheld in all its strength. In the *Prinz von Homburg* Kleist produced his best and last work. All the brilliant characteristics, which make his figure stand out prominently from the great crowd of dramatists, he displayed in this work as never before and combined them with full mastery over all artistic devices. His power as a poet was still increasing when despair and an intolerable disgust of life drove him, on Nov. 21, 1811, into voluntary death.

In his lifetime only *Der zerbrochene Krug* and *Käthchen von Heilbronn* were put upon the stage. Kleist's fame blossomed late and even then his attempt to create a realistic drama met with but little real appreciation. The field belonged to the false idealism of the descendants of classicism.

THE IMITATORS OF SCHILLER.

With the works of his last period Schiller had won his greatest triumphs, because he combined in ideal excellence suitable stage-technique with great thought-content, unerring judgment with inspiring flights of poetry. It did not seem difficult to appropriate this style which offered so many advantages. The preponderance of incident over characterization anticipated the delight of the public in external agencies, in stage effects. The action is under the guidance of a higher power outside the play. This exercises an inexorable influence over great characters who think themselves free and fight against it with all their might. And yet the individual case appears as a type of human destiny. In the characterization of his personages he preferred great and easily comprehended outlines and avoided everything complicated, inexplicable and disordered. His language is full of grand and brilliant metaphors which sacrifice pithiness to beauty and is rich in interpolations of generalized truths and aphorisms. The subjects are taken from the history of the Middle Ages or of modern times and offer plenty of occasion for varied and figure-filled canvases. The iambic pentameter seemed easy to master and gave dignity to the dialogue which, by help of the rhyme at the climaxes, attained increased melodious effect.

All these superficial qualities of Schiller's later dramas have been copied faithfully for nearly a century by his imitators and they have supposed that thereby they possessed a style in lofty drama which would hold good for all time. But they forgot in doing this that only Schiller's peculiar personality gave these forms their validity and disguised their lack of unity and modern consciousness. Schiller's great judgment in matters of history had comprehended in every case the true significance of the scenes he portrayed, his great genius had given form in brilliant language to an ideal, self-acquired world of thought. The power of his characterization had, in defiance of his own artificially constructed principles, almost everywhere revealed the inner just as fully as the outward causes of the destinies and deeds of his heroes. The breath of inspiration exhaled from his dramas carried all before it and corresponded to that ethical idealism which soon afterwards, disjoined from other ideas, became a mere phrase with later writers. It was a fateful error when it was generally believed that one could not improve on Schiller and must strive for his effect and with his means.

Even in young THEODOR KÖRNER these characteristics are conspicuous in his first dramas, *Toni, Zriny, Hedwig, Rosamunde* (all 1812). As a writer of comedies he follows Kotzebue, whom he also resembles in his rapid and frivolous methods of work. He possessed a decided sense for theatrical effects and would doubtless have given to the German stage a number of successful, even though inherently unimportant works, had not a heroic death for the Fatherland fallen to his lot.

Without the stage-skill of Körner, the noble LUDWIG UHLAND could not, with all his efforts, win any success as a dramatist, in spite of his higher poetic gifts. The only representatives of his numerous sketches which appeared in print, *Ernst, Herzog von Schwaben* (1818) and *Ludwig, der Bayer* (1819) brought no gain to the stage. The same thing happened to a number of dilettanti who expressed noble ideas in their dramas without the necessary mastery of technique, such as FRIEDRICH VON UCHTRITZ, EDWARD VON SCHENK, and MICHAEL BEER. Directors of theatres and actors, such as AUGUST KLINGEMANN and FRANZ VON HOLBEIN, who with shrewd calculation understood how to employ Schiller's style gained a great public. The greatest success in this way was won by ERNST RAUPACH, a prosaic, cool, calculating, common sense writer, who for a time dominated the stage with his worthless tragedies and comedies.

FRANZ GRILLPARZER.

The one great dramatist whom Germany possessed at Schiller's death, Heinrich von Kleist, died unheeded by his contemporaries. The whole energy of the nation was turned to the one thought of deliverance from the yoke of Napoleon and, when after a great and heroic struggle it was finally accomplished, when this mighty restless spirit was banished to St. Helena, every one hoped for a period of freedom. Never was a hope more shamefully deceived. What the sword had won, the pen destroyed. The princes forgot the promises which in time of need they had made to their subjects. Matters looked worst of all in Austria. For centuries the Hapsburgs had seen in Jesuitism the means of holding together and ruling their disunited peoples. In the short reign of Joseph II alone was a more liberal spirit displayed. "Good" Emperor Franz returned to the old paths, the Jesuits again received charge of

public instruction; the cloisters and other institutions
secularized by the state were again established and the
police supervision of Metternich threatened all independent thought with the severest punishment.

FRANZ GRILLPARZER, the ablest of those who followed
in the footsteps of Goethe and Schiller, had to live
and write in this Austria of Metternich's. Where they
had stood he would have preferred to stand, for he
thought that the world would need several generations
to rise to the height of their idealism. But, to-day we
must say it was fortunate for him, his gentle nature
was not strong enough to overcome the earthly, and
therefore his creations could not disown the influence
of the soil and of the time in which they had their
origin.

He first saw the light of day in Vienna on Jan. 15,
1791. The tenacious uprightness and clear judgment of
his father, the passionate, musical and nervous nature
of his mother were united in him. This mingling of
the opposite natures of the parents made Grillparzer
a peculiar, contradictory, perverse and yet weak-willed
character. Only a small measure of freedom and favorable circumstances would have been necessary to let
him find the way to the cheerful regions of peace and
good fortune. His nature and his talents continually
sought peace and beauty; and yet from youth up he
was sinned against by the education and the environment in which he grew to manhood. When he had finished his studies, after a distressing existence as a
private tutor, he received a position in the Civil service
in which he was obliged to remain until 1856. The
fame which he won as a writer was fatal to him in this
position and hindered his advancement. As an official

he was not taken at his full value and was considered a suspicious character in the Austria of that day, as was every one whose independent spirit aimed to attain to higher things. Therefore he was obliged in the days of his best powers to carefully repress every expression of independence and was never sure but that the life of his intellectual offspring would be stifled even in the cradle by a stupid censorship. He became a discontented, embittered man. Not understood by the easy-going, happy-spirited Viennese, he lived in solitude beside the love of his youth to whom he had never dared to unite himself because he lacked courage to believe in good fortune. The Revolution of 1848 brought the possibility of freedom to write and his almost forgotten works were revived through the instrumentality of Laube; but that did not become in him a joyous incitement to new activity because his desire to create had died in him. He lived on until Jan. 21, 1872, but during this long period produced scarcely anything new.

Grillparzer first appeared to the public as an author when twenty-five years of age. His first acted drama, *Die Ahnfrau* (1816), was a fate-tragedy in spite of the fact that the poet denied this. It did, indeed, stand high above the seemingly similar plays of Müllner by whom it was most influenced; not with cool calculation but with glowing passion did the poet transform the contents of a penny-dreadful into a genuine and great work of art. With him the hereditary impulse to evil, which may lie in the blood, does not do away with moral responsibility. In this way *Die Ahnfrau* is distinguished from the rest of the fate-tragedies as well as from the heredity-plays of the present. Moreover, it is not a question with him, as with his predecessors, of revealing former events; on the contrary, an action developing with astonishing rapidity in the presence of the spectators compels the attention of all. And thus *Die Ahnfrau,* which quickly made Grillparzer's name famous all over Germany, has also justly outlived the vogue of the fate-tragedies.

His second tragedy, *Sappho* (1818), forms the strongest contrast to *Die Ahnfrau.* In the latter he borrowed the material from the field of the robber-and-ghost-romances and the passionate pathos from Schiller's early dramas; in the former Goethe's *Iphigenie* was his model and he endeavored to attain to classic and refined beauty. His characters are just as noble as those of Goethe but their movements are more animated and their acts proceed rather from the accidental conditions of a peculiar personality. The heroine, Sappho, is to perish because of the variance between her calling as an artist and the longings of her passionate woman's nature. And yet the poet did not succeed in giving this conflict convincing form, for in the catastrophe she is in reality only a jealous woman in love and absorbed in her passion, a woman who loves a younger man. Phaon, deceiving himself, believes he loved the admired artist but recognizes his mistake when the lovely Melitta comes into his ken. In this couple we see, for the first time in Grillparzer's works, an awakening through love out of a dreamy existence to a life full of action. Though *Die Ahnfrau,* because of its affinity to the fate-tragedies and in spite of its success, did meet with opposition from the critics, the poet was now recognized because of Sappho as the greatest among those who had appeared since the classic writers.

A brilliant future seemed to be opening up before him

and with glad heart he began the creation of a third work, *Das goldene Vliess,* which was to far surpass the two preceding in range and importance. The extended treatment necessitated three parts, although Grillparzer himself recognised that the mutual dependence of one part on the others would give to the whole something of an epic effect, by means of which it would probably gain in individuality but lose in truth and pithiness.

When the first part, *Der Gastfreund,* and the first three acts of the second, *Die Argonauten,* had been finished in the brief period between Sept. 29 and Nov. 3, 1818, the suicide of his mother interrupted the activities of the poet for a long time and only in 1820 was the work completed by the addition of the last part, *Die Medea.* In spite of this, the long-drawn-out composition possesses a complete, well-knit, intrinsic unity. The fleece, as an outward sign of what is desirable and eagerly sought after but unrighteously gained, ruins all its possessors, not, however, as the result of a curse attached to it, but as Jason says:

> " Nicht gut, nicht schlimm ist, was die Götter geben,
> Und der Empfänger erst macht das Geschenk.
> So wie das Brot, das uns die Erde spendet,
> Den Starken stärkt, des Kranken Siechtum mehrt,
> So sind der Götter hohe Gaben alle,
> Dem Guten gut, dem Argen zum Verderben."

Medea, the heroine of the trilogy, develops from a naïve child of nature, in whom savagery and tenderness form a peculiarly fascinating mixture, into a deserted woman thirsting for revenge. She murders her own children in order to take vengeance on Jason, an outwardly pleasant but unimpassioned egoist. The contrast between barbaric, unbridled impulse and Hellenic culture forms the background and is another source of the tragic fate of the heroine.

Once more only did Grillparzer go back to classic antiquity, in the tragedy, *Des Meeres und der Liebe Wellen* (1831), when he made the same subject which Schiller had treated in his ballad, *Hero und Leander,* the basis of a drama. While Schiller makes the bold youth who ventures everything for the possession of his loved one the hero, Grillparzer glorifies in Hero love itself. This constitutes the conflict and the tragic subject. In Hero all is bright and unconscious. Not a moment does she reflect on the righteousness of her action; the most gracious charm encircles her; her nature is thoroughly transparent and sensible, but in her soul there glimmers an uncertain, ominous light. The style approaches that of the comedy with its many finely executed touches and its outward calm, which makes the fear of approaching fate flare up at certain points only the more threateningly.

This same mixture, even if in a somewhat different proportion, is shown in the fairy-play, *Der Traum ein Leben* (1834). The technique of the scenes, passing by in vehement rapidity, is successfully caught from a dream and the whole dipped in the gay colors of Oriental splendor. Greatness is recognised as dangerous, Fame as an idle game:

> " Was er giebt, sind nichts als Schatten,
> Was er nimmt, es ist so viel."

How deeply this conviction was rooted in Grillparzer's breast, is shown by his peculiar plan for the continuation of the first part of Goethe's *Faust.* After Gretchen's terrible catastrophe Faust was to take thought with himself and so find in what happiness really consists; in self-limitation and peace of mind. This draft remained undeveloped but *König Ottokars Glück und Ende* (1825) promulgated the same doctrine of the ruin which follows unbridled desire. Beside Ottokar, who in many of his characteristics reminds one of Napoleon, there appeared as his superior opponent, Rudolf Hapsburg, the founder of the Austrian Imperial dynasty. With warm patriotism Grillparzer pictured him in his simple, capable, unassuming manliness and thus to the injury of the drama diverted interest from the fate of Ottokar. Here alone has he pictured that passion, otherwise treated most frequently by modern dramatists, viz: lust for power. Those conflicts appealed more strongly to him which interfered rather with the fine emotions and the solution of which is dependent upon the peculiar nature of the characters concerned.

For this reason the character and moral conflict of the Palatine Bankbanus had an attraction for him. But in spite of all the charm which the problem and its psychological treatment possesses in the play, *Ein treuer Diener seines Herrn* (1828), there is after all something painful and whimsical in it, because the servant's faithfulness gains the victory over more worthy human characteristics and because one can only with difficulty put himself in the place of Bankbanus. And yet the poet succeeded in the delineation of two figures, the beautiful female character Ernys and the arrogant mad Otto von Meran, which are counted among the most original in all German dramatic literature. The drama was played in Vienna, Feb. 28, 1828, amid storms of applause, but immediately afterwards forbidden, probably because a popular revolt is described, and in spite of the fact that the spirit of Metternich's time, the spirit of implicit obedience, found in the play its most brilliant artistic expression.

No wonder that creative work became distasteful to the poet. Finally he desisted entirely from offering his contemporaries new gifts when his comedy, *Weh' dem, der lügt,* at its first production in 1838 was rejected by the stupid audience of the *Burg-theater* at Vienna. In place of the usual shallow drollery of comedy there appears in this work a theme of serious importance to humanity, and the treatment is bright and masterly. The conditional nature of all human action, which must not make claim to perfection, is seen in the examples of the bold, lovable, wily scullion Leon and of the wise and extremely kind but unsophisticated Bishop Gregory von Tours. Once more the worlds of culture and of barbarism are contrasted with each other. The rude ludicrous tricks, by which the boorish Germans are characterized, excited for a long time the greatest surprise, until the genuine poetry and great merit of this comedy were recognized, for it stands alone in its class.

Grillparzer had still more than a generation to live, but the few works which were produced in this period remained locked up in the poet's desk because he did not wish to expose himself to the fickle judgment of a public which had made him uncertain of himself. In his will he devised that two of his most valuable dramas should be burned after his death; *Ein Bruderzwist in Habsburg* and *Libussa.* Granted that the first of these works is rightly considered ineffective, the author has at least produced in Emperor Rudolf II his most finely conceived tragic figure. *Libussa* must, as symbolic poetry, win more and more recognition, the farther the knowledge extends that the greatest problems of poetry lie entirely within the field of the symbolic. What was prominent before in *Das goldene Vliess* and in *Weh' dem, der lügt*—significant indeed but not a chief theme—the representation of mankind in the transition from unconscious, instinct-impelled existence to conscious willing and doing, this is in this play in the dress of the fairy-story, so developed that the pain of departing from a purely natural existence and the blessings of the new and richer life of a more highly evolved humanity appear in the same warm pure light of historical knowledge.

The *Jüdin von Toledo,* too, did not become known until after the death of the author. Having its origin in a play by the Spaniard, Lope de Vega, whom Grillparzer honored very highly in his old age, he represented the youthful, well-trained king as consumed by passion for the cold, sensual, mendacious Jewess who is endowed with all the charms of an original unexhausted nature. He is completely enslaved. But he soon awakens sobered from his excesses. He is ashamed of his weakness and when the Jewess, murdered by the queen and her partisans, lies lifeless before him, her charm is also completely destroyed. And yet the king recognizes that in her was Truth, "for everything that she did proceeded from herself, suddenly, unexpectedly and without precedent."

The *Jüdin von Toledo* takes rank deservedly with the earlier female characters of Grillparzer, charming because of their unconsciousness. That the seeds of evil and of crime grow in such a creature under the covering of a most attractive lovableness was to be made manifest in *Esther*. Only the beginning of this drama was worked out by Grillparzer, but the great love-scene between Esther and King Ahasuerus is reckoned among the most beautiful in all poetry.

Grillparzer considered it the goal of his dramatic authorship to be varied and life-like down to the smallest detail, and yet at the same time never to lose sight of the underlying thought. In his diary he once called himself "that middle thing between Goethe and Kotzebue which the times need" and if, at his own valuation, he does place himself too low, he has indeed and in truth, without allowing the great main lines of humanity to vanish entirely, observed better than the classic writers the small curiously drawn arabesques of personages and times, while at the same time he acceded to the demand for external theatrical effect. For this reason his work is far more closely related to the tendencies of the authors of the present day, especially in his later dramas, than he himself suspected; also in this, that it is influenced most strongly by his native city Vienna and by the art of its people.

The latter also, shows the same fresh appeal to the senses, the same delight in little carefully observed characteristics, the same lack of productive energy. But the pleasure-loving Viennese were entirely hostile to anything over-subtle and did not want to know anything of the great problems of life.

FERDINAND RAIMUND

The theater in the suburb, Leopoldstadt, was the home of the folk-writers of Vienna, who incarnated the gay naïve disposition of the lower classes in scenes from the life of their beautiful Imperial city. Following the old traditions of the Renaissance tragedy and the opera they made gods and spirits appear at the same time in their plays. Everything was calculated for comic effect; longer than anywhere else in Germany the clown here prolonged his dominion.

For this stage FERDINAND RAIMUND wrote his plays. He was the son of a turner, born June 1, 1790, received a brief schooling and was then apprenticed to a confectioner. At eighteen he went on the stage and from 1817–1830 played comic parts in the theater of the Leopoldstadt. As actor, he won for himself from the first general popularity. He first supplemented and revised the plays in which he acted. Then he composed, entirely in the style of the old Viennese extravaganza, his first play, *Der Barometermacher auf der Zauberinsel* (1823). The next was already somewhat more· independent, *Der Diamant des Geisterkönigs* (1824). His attempt to give a somewhat greater seriousness to the form of the fairy-play produced something new and more valuable in *das Mädchen aus der Feenwelt oder der Bauer als Millionär* (1826). This is a picture of a typical destiny deduced from a character likewise of the nature of a type. Grillparzer was right in congratulating Austria that the healthy sense of the nation could produce such graceful plays. He says pertinently that Raimund's half unconscious gift has its root in the spirit of the masses.

Grillparzer ascribes it to the injudicious zeal of well-meaning friends that Raimund attempted to leave the broad ground of the popular play. But the ambition of the artist, with all his personal modesty, his great respect for higher culture, for him no longer attainable, and his serious, indeed, gloomy disposition had certainly the chief part in the change that now took place in his creations.

When Raimund, after a severe illness, put *Die gefesselte Phantasie* (1826) and *Moisasurs Zauberfluch* (1827) on the stage, he clothed serious problems in the usual gay magical scenes and sought to attain the style of great tragedy. But it was not a success, because a labored unnatural style had taken the place of natural simplicity and the cheery element indispensable to folk-pieces had been forcibly repressed. Therefore Raimund turned again to the manner of his first plays and with ripened powers wrote his best works: *Der Alpenkönig und der Menschenfeind* (1828) and *Der Verschwender* (1833). The self-tormenting misanthrope had already shown the increasing melancholy of the author who ended his life by suicide, Sept. 5, 1836. With him came to an end also the old Viennese folk-play with its innocent, cheerful mirth and its soulful poetry; even in Raimund's day a talented but unscrupulous author had arisen in JOHANN NESTROY who now for thirty years ruled the stage of Vienna's suburbs and made it a wrestling place for sharp satire, bold parody, frivolous sensuality and the greatest absurdities.

PLAY AND COMEDY (1800–1830)

When in 1800 Schiller and Goethe offered a prize
for a bright play suitable for the stage, thirteen works
were sent in. Not a single one could be used, the
greater number were beneath criticism. Each and
every author who provided for the daily needs of the
stage was a follower of Kotzebue. For the most part
they were players and directors of theatres, such as
KARL TÖPFER, who wrote *Hermann und Dorothea* (1820),
Des Königs Befehl (1821), *Der Pariser Taugenichts*
(1839), *Rosenmüller und Finke* (1850); PIUS ALEXAN-
DER WOLFF, the follower of Goethe in *Preziosa* (1821);
KARL BLUM, who imported the short opera, called vaudeville, from France, and composed numerous comedies
in Kotzebue's manner, such as *Ich bleibe ledig* (1835),
Der Ball zu Ellerbrunn (1835), *Erziehungsresultate*
(1840).

More successful than all the stage writers of the
male sex in their day were the two actresses, JOHANNA
VON WEISSENTHURN and CHARLOTTE BIRCH-PFEIFFER.
The wretched plays and comedies of the former with
their disguises and intrigues, their airy speeches and
sentimentality were long in highest favor with the
public. The latter, after great success on the stage,
turned her attention from 1828 to dramatising popular
novels and stories, as for example, *Der Glöckner von
Notredame* after Victor Hugo (1837), *Dorf und Stadt*
after Berthold Auerbach, *Die Waise aus Lowood* after
Charlotte Bronte (1856), *Die Grille,* after George Sand
(1860). With most unerring judgment she took from
her "copy" everything that would contribute to outward effect on the stage and wrote most acceptable

rôles for the players. She understood how to make her plays affecting and exciting, just such as the great body of the public demanded, and thus won triumphs which in duration and number are scarcely to be surpassed.

At all times the folk-play and the lower type of drama have occasionally used dialect to produce comic effect. Through the influence of the Romanticists, dialect, so long despised, once more attained a high degree of literary importance and the drama now began to make use of it, no longer exclusively for the purpose of amusement but also as a means of delineating character.

DANIEL ARNOLD wrote in the Strassburg dialect his *Pfingstmontag* (1816), a work which Goethe justly admired. KARL MALSZ sketched the rough peculiarities of the Frankfort people in numberless local plays with stock-figures, as *Der alte Bürgerkapitän* (1820). LOUIS ANGELY delineated the people of Berlin in the twenties just as inoffensively and kindly as Raimund did the Viennese, though with more modest poetic talent, e. g., *Das Fest der Handwerker* (1828); JÜRGEN NIKLAS BÄRMANN composed his Hamburg *Burenspillen,* and his fellow-countryman, JAKOB HEINRICH DAVID, wrote local farces which were long popular, such as *Eine Nacht auf Wache* (1835). All the writers named contented themselves with cautiously avoiding all offence to the higher classes and sketching good and bad in their fellow countrymen. The critics ventured at most to attack municipal authorities and regulations. Just in this very thing can be seen how portentous for the drama was the oppression which, after the War of Liberation, was exercised in Germany. The play was supervised more solicitously than any other class of literature.

And yet the theatre meant then, as always in times of political decadence, compensation to the educated classes for the part denied them in public life. That enthusiasm which was not allowed to take an active part in public affairs was kindled and consumed in the enjoyment of inferior writings and of the performances of actors whose importance was vastly over-rated. When one reads the criticisms of Tieck and Ludwig Börne, one is astonished at the lack of critical judgment against which they had continually to fight. The great works of Schiller and Goethe appeared but rarely and like those of Shakespeare became the sport of the "star" actor who, lacking all reverence, destroyed the very framework of these noble productions for the sake of external effect.

The efforts of managers of artistic taste, such as Schreyvogel in Vienna and Immermann in Düsseldorf, were but little honored even in individual cases and had no influence at all upon other theatres, in spite of the fact that the means for a proper artistic staging were now oftener at hand because of the establishment of numerous court and city theatres.

CHRISTIAN DIETRICH GRABBE

There was no place in these theatres for such a fantastical genius as that of CHRISTIAN DIETRICH GRABBE. He was born at Detmold, Dec. 1, 1801, brought up in poor circumstances as the son of the superintendent of a house of correction and while a student wrote his first work, *Herzog Theodor von Gothland* (1822). When completed he sent it to Tieck and demanded that he brand him publicly as an impertinent and wretched poetaster if he found his tragedy similar to the products of the usual writers of the day. In this utterance is seen his mania for departing from the customary and it put its stamp upon his first as well as on all his later dramas. They are alive with bold cynicism, untamed caprice but also with great and genuine passion. There is also the play of brilliant humor, profound contempt for the world and insolent arrogance in the comedy, *Scherz, Satire, Ironie und tiefere Bedeutung* (1822), and it cannot be staged at all.

In his birthplace Grabbe got a small position and in new work rose to clearer heights. *Don Juan und Faust* (1824), a bold attempt to contrast with one another these two representatives of the strongest sensual and intellectual desires, was free from the earlier outbreaks of affected titanism. In the two tragedies, *Kaiser Friedrich Barbarossa* (1829) and *Kaiser Heinrich VI* (1830), he succeeded, with far greater ability than his numerous competitors, in comprehending the spirit of history and the mighty figures of the rulers from the race of the Hohenstaufens. But here already is seen the style of presenting a series of scarcely connected and hastily sketched gigantic frescoes instead of a uniform dramatic picture.

This manner amounts to the grotesque in Grabbe's most important work, *Napoleon oder die hundert Tage* (1831). He makes whole battlefields his stage and despises all the requirements of dramatic writing, but he gives historic pictures of true grandeur and great distinctness. What Grabbe later composed, *Hannibal, Aschenbrödel, Die Hermannsschlacht,* shows that the vice of drink had already deranged his mind even though in many places traces of his original power were still visible. His early death, Sept. 12, 1836, released him from an existence which was a failure because of an unfortunate disposition and lack of will-power.

In his article on *Shakespearomania* (1827), in opposition to the blind admirers and imitators of Shakespeare, Grabbe says, ''The German nation wants the greatest possible simplicity and clearness in language, form and plot, it wants to feel in tragedy an unbroken inspiration, it wants to find true and deep emotion, it wants a national and at the same time a genuinely dramatic historical play, it wants not English but German characters, it wants strong language and good verse and in the comic scenes, it demands, not peculiar turns or witticisms, which except for the form of expression have nothing witty in them, but sound common sense, a wit that strikes every time like lightning, a poetic and moral power.'' Finally he mentioned Schiller as the writer who best answered to these requirements. One sees, however, how unreliable Grabbe's judgment is when he calls Müllner's *Schuld* and *König Ingurd* the most satisfactory works since Schiller's death.

Grabbe did not attempt in any way to meet in his own dramas the requirements he mentions. With his striving after a faithful reproduction of reality and his contempt of all ideals, he may be considered one of the precursors of that trend which later took a position hostile to classic and romantic poetry.

Grabbe had as contemporary GEORG BÜCHNER, who, as a naturalist, proclaimed the absolute necessity of all that happens being considered as under the dominion of the laws of nature, as for instance in his drama *Danton's Tod* (1835), in his posthumous comedy *Leonce und Lena* and in the fragment *Wozzek*. Everywhere he aimed at transferring the world of reality without change into his artistic production. Like most naturalists he was attracted only by the dark sides of life which he reproduced with the keenest powers of observation in all their particulars, even the most repulsive. Later ALBERT DULK pursued a similar course in his dramas *Orla* (1844), *Simson* (1859) and *Jesus der Christ* (1865); also ROBERT GRIEFENKERL in *Maximilian Robespierre* (1851) and *Die Girondisten* (1852).

ROMANTIC OPERA.

The musical drama was created in Italy at the end of the sixteenth century, for the purpose of reviving, by the use of an elevated recitative, the solemn effect of the Greek tragedy, but it soon became the prey of stars of the singing world and of the desire for display. Later the genius of GLUCK restored again the original character of the opera and at the same time there developed from the modest operetta that style which, uniting an attractive appeal to the senses with great dramatic passion, found in MOZART its master and greatest exponent. After his death this style degenerated in Germany into humdrum Philistinism and sentimentality, while the great French and Italian masters, such as Méhul, Cherubini, Rossini and Auber, were trying to unite the dignity of Gluck with the inimitable sublime charm of Mozart.

Only one immortal opera in classic style was written during this time in Germany, Beethoven's *Fidelio*, the text of which, adapted at first by Joseph Sonnleithner and then by Friedrich Treitschke, effectively glorified conjugal fidelity in the simplest dramatic form. Three times revised, this, the only opera by Beethoven, received its final form in 1814. It combines chaste grandeur and warm genuine feeling within its strictly drawn outlines.

Although there was still found in classic opera a number of noble masters such as LOUIS SPOHR, and in comic opera such a successful talent as ALBERT LORTZING who wrote *Zar und Zimmermann* (1837), and *Der Waffenschmied* (1845), yet after all the leadership fell from now on to the Romanticists. The longing to express the unconscious, the delight in musical effects, the dislike to reasonable clearness—all this went to make music one of the fundamentals of the art of Romantic writers and while they had tried in vain to win success in spoken drama, the German opera of the nineteenth century became permeated with their spirit and chose its materials from their favorite fields, the fairy-story, German legend and the life of the Middle Ages.

CARL MARIA VON WEBER was the creator of the Romantic opera. In the year 1821 he finished his *Freischütz*, for which Friedrich Kind had written the text according to a Bohemian legend as told by Apel. The national character of the subject, the richness of melody, and the employment of new and highly impressive means of instrumentation prepared the way for the immense success of the *Freischütz*, by which means it gained the ascendancy over the prevailing Italian art and has remained the most popular German opera down to the present day.

Weber in this work had already made use of recurring themes, for the purposes of characterization, and began to do away with the endless arias which destroyed dramatic connection and to employ those freer recitatives which are on the border-line between song and declamation. The dramatic element, represented up to that time by the language alone, had played but an unimportant part; now it appeared in the music on an equality with the melody. At the same time greater demands were made on the acting skill of the singers. The orchestra now no longer served the purpose of giving body and greater fulness of tone by its accompaniment, but it began, with its explanations and supplements, to develop independently alongside the singing voices and in its own purely instrumental movements to become a significant factor of the opera.

A second great work of Weber's, *Euryanthe* (1823), unsuccessful, indeed, because of the unfavorable subject, was still farther removed from the old-style opera by its exact declamation and the strong emphasis laid on characterization and on dramatic passion. In these matters it showed still more clearly the road leading to the art of Richard Wagner.

Between Weber and Wagner the link is HEINRICH MARSCHNER. In his *Hans Heiling* (1833) we hear, in addition to the strains of the *Freischütz*, the advance notes of the *Fliegende Holländer*.

In the meantime the so-called *"Grand Opera"* had developed in France and Italy. It originated, as did the German romantic opera, in an opposition to the quiet, dispassionate art of the classic writer and chose its subjects from the same domains as the former; it did not aim, however, at plunging into the unexplored depths of the soul nor at portraying the mysterious workings of nature, but, by the use of strong and visible passion, did aim at arousing at all costs powerful emotion. In the choice of subjects and of artistic expedients it therefore followed the like-minded Romantic writers of the French. It dazzled by an accumulation of all effects that appeal to the senses, it offered a full, exciting though often quite senseless plot and brilliant stage-scenes to which an extrinsic grandeur was given by massive music and crowds of actors; it anticipated all the lower instincts of singers and public and ruthlessly destroyed unity and truth by interjecting showy songs and ballets.

As in the old Italian opera so here the drama was only an excuse for the satisfaction of curiosity and of the vulgar passion for unusual performances of the singing voice. But more cunningly than their predecessors the composers of "Grand Opera" and their complaisant text-writers succeeded in concealing these purposes from a shortsighted public by an appearance of dramatic unity.

The most noteworthy representative of this art was JACOB MEYERBEER. He had constant success from *Robert der Teufel* (1831) and *Die Hugenotten* (1836) down to his last work *die Afrikanerin* which was first played in the year after his death (1864). All this time he dominated the German as well as the French operatic stage.

Only when one recognizes the pernicious influence of Meyerbeer upon the German public, does one comprehend the passionate wrath with which all, who had the opera seriously at heart, fought against him. At their head stand Robert Schumann and Peter Cornelius, who, with their weak dramatic talents, tried in vain to win the stage back to pure art, and Richard Wagner, the victor in this strife.

GERMAN DRAMA FROM 1830–85

YOUNG GERMANY AND ITS FOLLOWERS

The fifty-five years from 1830–85 present a picture of the condition of the German drama outwardly similar to that of the preceding period. Schiller remains, with few exceptions, the only model for tragedy, and the tradition of Romanticism continues with decreasing influence until it gradually dies out. The great changes in the political and social conditions of Germany do not find expression on the stage. The greatest writers of the times, who are aiming at a new art suited to their day, are scarcely noticed and gain no influence over the production of the others or the taste of the spectators. The German drama keeps sinking lower and lower to a powerless decadence. The theatre becomes more and more the home of hollow phrases and shallow entertainment while the belief in the exclusive rights of the idealizing form is strenuously upheld. Musical drama alone reaches the highest point of its development through the mighty creative work of Richard Wagner.

How little it was possible in this period to convert the correct perception of the artistic needs of the present into deeds is shown by the example of that group of writers brought together under the name, *Das junge Deutschland*. They represented in general the demands of the Liberals in Paris in the July-revolution of 1830 and opposed the romanticist alienation from life and reality as well as all false idealism and visionary caprice. LUDOLF WIENBARG, the æsthetic authority of "Young Germany," insists upon the treatment of subjects true to and full of life and emphasizes above all what is important for the present of any particular time. The place of poetic fancy is to be taken by that enthusiasm which inspires to deeds. The Middle Ages have outlived themselves and a protest is made against dead and hollow formulas and also against the attempts to regenerate the present with the help of the ancient. From the drama Wienbarg demands national spirit but not in the form of nature poetry, as the Romanticists made it, but as a work of art with a democratic trend, filled with the idea of a body of free citizens who had become of age in a political sense. His second requirement was that the contents should be national and yet not in the historical form of Goethe's and Schiller's works and those of their successors. For poetry is not dramatized history and national contents do not depend upon national and historical material but upon the fact that they are interesting and valuable for the whole nation, that is, are national in the true sense. From this is derived the third requirement of contents suited to the times. The youth are to fight on against the tenacity and opposition of reactionary efforts in all departments and begin with what the "Storm and Stress" writers strove for and in the same sense.

These requirements were met only in a very small degree by the "Young Germany" writers, Heine, Laube, Gutzkow, in their dramatic works. Heine was never again active as a dramatic writer after his first abortive attempts, Laube and Gutzkow were both too very eager for stage effect to place themselves by innovations in decided opposition to the prevailing taste.

This external theatrical technique, this cool scheming for effect which had scarcely been known before in Germany, at least in tragedy, was to be ascribed to the strong influence of French models. Victor Hugo and Alexander Dumas, *père,* at the head of the French Romanticists in historical drama, had taught them exaggerated delineation of character and inconsiderate working on the emotions of the public, while at the same time Eugène Scribe, aided by numerous contemporaneous playwrights, dominated the stages of Europe with his comedies. A fine outer polish, the greatest skill in all that was technical, complete lack of any deeper spirit, exciting intrigues, often carried out at the cost of reality, these are the attributes which mark Scribe. The influence of this thoroughly superficial but ever graceful and entertaining class of drama reaches down into the present and for a long time represented alone finer comedy in Germany.

HEINRICH LAUBE was the best judge of the theatre, the foremost manager whom Germany possessed in the nineteenth century. As director of the Burg-theatre in Vienna, he did a great work from 1849–66 in the training of the players and in the enlargement of the repertoire. But for the author those excellencies were fateful which stood the director in good stead. The mechanical nature of the effects was too much in the foreground and instead of creating men he saw only players guided by the invisible hand of the manager. Therefore the most of his dramas are to-day as good as forgotten. *Die Karlsschüler* (1841) alone is still played here and there, not because of its intrinsic merit but because young Schiller, the author of *Die Räuber,* is its hero; with it the tragedy, *Graf Essex* (1856), keeps its place because of some good rôles.

KARL GUTZKOW, too, strives after external effect but with greater talent and more genuine passion than the cool and prudent Laube. Gutzkow said to himself, "The theatre is to reconcile life with art and art with life"; "Put men on the boards who are taken not from past centuries but from the present, not from the Assyrians and Babylonians—no, from your own surroundings." But when his first attempts to present the inherent contrasts of the times upon the stage had failed, he turned again to historical drama and only in the choice of his subjects and in his judgments upon the conduct of his heroes did he permit the liberal viewpoint of "Young Germany" to be seen.

On the border line between the modern and the historical plays of Gutzkow stands his best work, *Uriel Acosta* (1847), changed from a short story to a drama of great elevation and genuine vitality. The conflict between liberal thought and positive dogma, between a sense of independence and of reverence, is here very effectively converted into a succession of scenes argued from a purely human standpoint; the characters, with the exception of the pale youthful Spinoza who comes in at the end, are drawn clearly and with life. This drama may therefore be characterized as the best of its kind, though it clearly shows the traces of decadence in its too strong pathos, its lack of characteristic shading in the language and in its delight in strong, stirring and extraneous incidents.

In the field of historical comedy Gutzkow also stands at the head of his contemporaries. *Zopf und Schwert*

(1844) does not do justice to the historical importance
of Friedrich Wilhelm I, the central figure of the play,
because the powerful, far-seeing monarch is degraded to
a blustering family tyrant; but the tone is well caught,
the intrigues are clever and exciting, after the style
of Scribe, the characters superficial indeed and yet not
inaccurately delineated, and there is no lack of that
deeper spirit which is just as indispensable in comedy
as in tragedy.   The higher signification of the whole
class is the subject of the comedy, *Das Urbild des
Tartuffe* (1847).   It does not equal *Zopf und Schwert*
in outward effect but its artistic merit is greater.

While these two works are now very unjustly neglected and only rarely considered by the stage, *Der
Königsleutnant* (1849) has held its ground up to the
present.   It was originally merely destined to celebrate
the centennial of Goethe's birth and the author says
in his preface by way of excuse: "Opportunity is the
stepsister of the Muse."   He knew very well that he
had not offered in this play a work of art, but thanks
to an effective rôle, the favor of actors has prolonged
the life of this mawkish sentimental play far beyond
its own inherent vitality.

Dependent upon the French or their "Young German" imitators were a number of other dramatists
whose works attracted the public because of their strong
scenic effects and themes acceptable to the actors.   To-
day they are all rightly forgotten, the most successful
of them alone, EMIL BRACHVOGEL'S *Narziss* (1856), not
having yet quite lost its attractiveness for travelling
"stars."   The charm exercised by this degenerate genius
with his philosophical paradoxes and his despairing
humor, as well as the interesting condition of French

society before the Revolution, are made the most of for the sake of effect. But there is a lack of all deeper conception of the spirit of the times and of the historical personages introduced; in their conversations they represent the political tendencies of liberalism and the materialism, colored by natural science, of the author's own times.

In comedy the clever technique of the style of Scribe could be better preserved than in serious drama, especially where a stronger temper broke through the outward polish and coldness of the French models. In this way EDWARD VON BAUERNFELD succeeded in delineating skilfully and ably, kindly and feelingly, the society of Vienna. As with the French so also with him there is a graceful vivacity in the conversations. A fine cultivation of mind is revealed in the spontaneity of his wit, in his fear of the trivial; a strong common sense, enthusiasm for freedom and a cheery optimism give his works their glow and make it possible to overlook the theatrical artifices which he, too, does not disdain for the sake of success. With his comedy *Bürgerlich und Romantisch* (1835), which shows all the best characteristics of the author, he reached the climax of his powers; among his numerous dramas *Die Bekenntnisse* (1834), *Grossjährig* (1846), and *Ein deutscher Krieger* (1847) are also of a superior order.

From the French GUSTAV FREYTAG also learned what is best in his dramatic technique. In his first comedy, *Die Brautfahrt oder Kunz von der Rosen* (1841), he allowed himself to be governed too much by the Romantic delight in the bright game of life without consideration for the demands of the stage; then he produced in *Die Valentine* (1846) a brightly colored play of intrigue which with all its cleverness was not successful because genuine dramatic power is lacking in the fundamental theme. The same thing is true, too, of *Graf Waldemar* (1850), which does not portray convincingly enough the conversion of a *blasé* worldling by the awakening of a genuine and noble love. With *Die Journalisten* (1853) alone did Freytag gain a great and lasting influence because he found in it the subject most suitable for his peculiar talent and his acquired powers. The political extremes, at that time occupying the centre of general interest instead of artistic and philosophical questions, are made use of with success; the vocation of the journalist is faithfully described in its ideal importance and from its dark sides, the whole giving a slightly idealized but yet not an indistinct picture of German life, sketched with a sure hand and finished with fresh colors here and there somewhat too indifferent and cool. It is a very great pity, but it shows Freytag's clear self-knowledge, that he did not determine to attempt something further in the domain of comedy after this so singular success. His one dramatic work of later origin, *Die Fabier* (1859), was a tragedy which represented the fall of a great Roman family in conflict with the needs of the newly organized state. This significant but singular play could not hold its place on the stage.

MIDDLE-CLASS COMEDY AND THE FARCE

Even after 1830 the majority of writers of German comedy were still following the methods of Iffland and Kotzebue. The consummation of a marriage in middle-class life, trade and the maintenance of an honorable, comfortable living is the sole question with these authors. The horizon is purposely narrowed as much as possible, and not a single glance wanders beyond the borders of the small town. For a long time there was not to be found in these plays a breath of modern times, with its railways and telegraphs, its export industries and its political contests. Especially the latter were passed over most carefully so as in no way to disturb the harmless doings of the townspeople. Therefore the ethical teachings of these plays grow more and more nervous, branding all independent expression of emotion as immoral. The sentiments are inherently mendacious and hypocritical, propriety is made the standard for the individual and all great disinterested actions and all independent striving to higher things meet with bitter hostility.

This seemingly innocent class of plays became in reality very dangerous and harmful, above all because they stood for a long time in the way of genuine art and because, worse than the French plays which were decried because of their immorality, they flattered the lower inclinations, the laziness of mind and the self-complacency of the German middle-classes. Down to the present day they continue unchanged, inwardly coarse and outwardly proper, except that corresponding to the change of public, their horizon has also apparently widened a little and instead of the houses of small merchants we now see the electric-lighted villas of wholesale manufacturers, councillors and merchant-princes.

At the first glance one cannot of course estimate this unfavorable influence in its whole extent, when one considers, for example, the plays of RODERICH BENEDIX, which seem to aim only at exciting hilarity especially by means of comic situations. At most one will get annoyed with the clumsy, stupid dialogue and smile at the lack of all finer details in the drawing of the characters, and the rude, axe-hewn plot. And yet the truth of what has been said will soon be acknowledged when one thinks of the immense numbers and the popularity of the works of this class which rob better ones of light and air. The differences in merit are scarcely sufficient to enable one to pick out individual names from the host of comedy-writers of the recent past who are for the most part stage-experts and often in no way lacking in talent. But public success gives some names a better sound, such as, for example, JEAN BAPTIST VON SCHWEITZER, JULIUS ROSEN and FRANZ VON SCHÖNTHAN. GUSTAV MOSER achieved the greatest effect with his somewhat finer judgment and light work. His farce, *Der Bibliothekar* (1878), verges on absurdity but to its advantage is distinguished by genuine fun from the weak hilarity of most of the middle-class comedies.

The so-called folk-plays are a grade lower in artistic merit. They take their characters from the people, for example, from the ranks of the mechanics and laborers, inclusive of the proletariat, and from the view-point of middle-class ignorance of the true life of these lower classes deal with the surface of this existence, the essence of which is falsely taken to be merely a longing for the comfort of the middle classes and an amusing lack of education and society manners. The "authors" suppose that they have found a proper style for this class when they forego all artistic care in plot and characterization and with the rudest mechanical technique preach an obtrusive philistine morality.

The actor and manager HUGO MÜLLER made a valuable gift in this line to the theatres of lower rank with his folk-play, *Von Stufe zu Stufe,* while ADOLF L'ARRONGE, who ranks a little higher, became a welcome helper of court and city theatres in the sterile seventies with his plays, *Mein Leopold* (1877), *Hasemanns Töchter* (1877) and *Doktor Klaus* (1878). An honorable disposition is the distinguishing feature of all his characters and to this especially, together with cheap and oft repeated expedients to produce effect, is owing the favor of sentimental people who believe that they hear in his plays the voice of the German folk-soul.

One must not confuse these folk-plays, a degenerate subdivision of the domestic play, with the farce (*Posse*) which, as a dramatic form of contemporary satire, has grown up in quite a different field. The Berlin spirit, strongly permeated with Jewish elements, was its fostering soil. Its ancestors were the writers of operettas and dialect-plays; its father was DAVID KALISCH. The loosely woven plot is intended to beget a very small measure of excitement, because it is only the framework upon which is hung one after another a mass of puns, comic situations and satirical references to events of the day, and these entirely conceal it. The form of couplets perfected by Kalisch joined these real gems of the farce into brilliant showy plays. In his hands they did not fall out of their setting and become, as they did later, an abuse. He also continued to aim at a connected characterization which often caricatured definite personages, and at an outward propriety. He possessed also a genuine, rich, sparkling humor. Only in AUGUST WEYRAUCH did Kalisch find a successor of somewhat equal rank. To-day the Berlin farce, his creation, is the prey of a nasty reckoning upon coarse sensuality; in it absurdity alone wields the sceptre and it is distinguished from the rude comic of the circus clown by its ribald expressions and the situations which excite the horse-laugh.

As in Berlin, so also everywhere the dialect and local play has degenerated. In Vienna, it experienced its greatest prosperity because of the stage-writers in Leopoldstadt, and here, in Nestroy's day and afterwards, many of the most productive and clever writers of the class arose, as for example, FRIEDRICH KAISER. But the exclusive purpose of diverting their unassuming public and of touching their emotions by the cheapest means, as well as blind local patriotism and the arbitrariness of individual favorite actors, had in the long run a completely destructive influence. There were indeed in the peasant plays of upper Bavaria the beginnings of an improvement in dramatic dialect-writing, but here also sentimentality, low comic and mere theatrical effect remain the characteristics of a tendency obnoxious to art and of theatrical unnaturalness only imperfectly disguised by a covering of naïve feeling and peasant rudeness.

The only truly dramatic works dipped in the colors of dialect went by unheeded. These were the comedies in the Darmstadt dialect, *Des Burschen Heimkehr oder der tolle Hund* (1837) and *Der Datterich* (1840), composed by the highly gifted but early degenerate ERNST

ELIAS NIEBERGALL. The second work especially is filled
with a genuine cynical humor, by which a ragged genius
is raised above the cleverly caricatured philistines who
do not notice how he is despising them while serving
as their jester. In this portrait Niebergall stands out
as the precursor of Gerhart Hauptmann's *College
Crampton,* which appeared over half a century later.
As a link between the two we have the great phenomenon
of LUDWIG ANZENGRUBER, who again raised German
dialect and folk-plays into the domain of art.

IDEALIZING DRAMA

In the high class theatres folk-plays and dialect-pieces
were entirely tabooed during this period. The prevailing art-ideal only permitted that to pass current which
created another and better world far removed from
reality and which showed the outward characteristics of
harmonious beauty. This limited view originated in
the days of the Classicists and Romanticists. The clarified serenity of Hellenism was present to their minds as
the final goal. Their longing for a more beautiful life
wished to find satisfaction in literature. Where a great
talent like Grillparzer's was at work with this end in
view, there were produced grand works which did not
lack inherent warmth and truth, but when lesser talents
aspired to the same thing the result was smooth outward form without substance and the power of life was
lacking in the shadowy forms. The tragical did not
arise in them from great inward antagonisms but from
external collisions, especially from the conflict of passion with the demands of prevailing custom and the
inertia of environment in which these two forces were

considered legitimate while passion *per se* already meant guilt.

Historical and legendary subjects were still by far in the majority and most of the writers thought they had done enough when they seized upon some traditional character or other, striking because of its unusual fate, divided its life into acts and scenes, emphasized strongly the climaxes of the course of events and conferred upon the hero those typical qualities by which his fate was humanly to be explained. The particular conditions of time and place, the more intimate relations of things to each other, all psychology that lay in the province of the unknown, was at the same time completely neglected. In spite of their efforts to obtain strong outward effects, these dramatists seldom attained to even a momentary success because most of them despised the mechanical rules of the stage or were unable to conjoin them with the demands of an idealizing art. Only here and there could a greater poetic content or the charm of the subject delude the audience into overlooking the dramatic faults. To-day the most of these dramas have sunk into oblivion or still eke out a miserable existence, thanks only to a reverence which is scarcely in place.

The most successful author of this group was Eligius Franz Joseph Freiherr von Münch-Bellinghausen, known by the pseudonym FRIEDRICH HALM. His very first work, *Griseldis* (1834), showed an author who was master of mechanical expedients. It captured every stage by its romantic subject, melodious language, sentimental feeling and mawkish mood-painting. Among his numerous later dramas *Der Sohn der Wildnis* (1842) had the greatest influence. The contrast between culture and barbarism which Grillparzer had comprehended in its depth is here used merely to celebrate, in the barbarian youth Ingomar, the easy victory of love over defiant manliness. This same favorite character in somewhat different costumes becomes Thumelikus of the *Fechter von Ravenna* (1854) which added to the earlier properties of Halm's art, as approved aids to a shallow success, the hollow pathos of a cheap patriotism and the pungent description of moral depravity. In the dramatic poem, *Wildfeuer* (1863), the improbability that the heroine had been brought up as a boy and remained unknown in this rôle almost to the close is gladly accepted for the benefit of the piquant effect of this change of sex.

Nevertheless Halm's plays show after all in certain scenes a happy invention; his language is often trivial but the verse is clever and runs well. He knows how to arouse feeling by the insertion of lyric passages and he is reckoned among the few representatives of German Art-drama who knew the stage and its requirements exactly.

SOLOMON HERMANN RITTER VON MOSENTHAL, who likewise lived in Vienna, was the surest master of technique but for him it was an end in itself. He exerted no influence in historical tragedy but in his pathetic peasant-play, *Deborah* (1848), he produced one of the most popular dramas of his time. The great conceptions of tolerance and self-control are here incorporated into effective scenes and touching situations and the rôle of heroine offered actresses for a long time a welcome opportunity to show all their arts.

Besides Halm and Mosenthal many an aspiring dramatist of this period ought probably to be mentioned, but no one would have attained great and lasting success with dramas of ideal form. Poetic endowment and clear recognition of the problems do not at all suffice to make good the lack of specific dramatic talent and ability.

The virile JULIUS MOSEN wished to look at history as "a struggle between opposing principles, in which the contending spirits purify and ennoble each other and so present and solve in the drama the highest problems of man here below" or he wished "to help history to free consciousness and raise it in its ideals as the ancients did with nature." And yet he was not able to translate these purposes into a work that would live, however little the best, *Heinrich der Finkler* (1836), *Herzog Bernhard* (1842) and *Der Sohn des Fürsten* (1842), lacked in greatness and historical judgment.

In the numerous dramas of RUDOLF VON GOTTSCHALL rhetorical diction is the most prominent characteristic. In his earlier efforts he is closely allied to "Young Germany," when in *Ulrich von Hutten* (1843) and *Robespierre* (1846), with great expenditure of energy, he pleads the cause of liberal aspirations and the rights of sensuousness. Later this tendency vanishes and he treats historical subjects. But this he does with deficient characterization and a strong dependence on Shakespeare and Schiller, as in *Mazeppa* (1855), *Katharina Howard* (1868), *Maria de Padilla* (1889), *Rahab* (1898), *Der Götze von Venedig* (1901). His greatest success is the comedy written on the model of Scribe, *Pitt und Fox* (1854).

JOSEPH WEIL VON WEILEN was influenced by noble purposes but was likewise no great dramatist. His talent, which was rather a lyrical one, would hardly have drawn him to historical drama, had it not been that in the judgment of that day in it alone the laurels of a great writer were to be won. To gain these he wrote his romantic tragedies, *Tristan* (1860) and *Der arme Heinrich* (1860), then a succession of works in which we find some splendid female characters, as in *Drahomira* (1867) and *Rosamunde* (1869). Whatever in them was lacking in merit and truth was made good to the spectators by the plastic power of the great tragic actress of Vienna, Charlotte Wolter. Without this same assistance the finer gifts of FRANZ NISSEL could not obtain recognition and at the end of his career he looked back on an unusually sad and wasted life. With all his noble qualities there was lacking in him and his works the power to succeed, in spite of the fact that public attention was drawn to him in 1878 when he received the Schiller prize for his drama *Agnes von Meran*.

Like Halm and Nissel, OSKAR VON REDWITZ may also be reckoned as a descendant of the Romanticists, only, however, as a degenerate one. His drama, *Philippine Welser* (1859), was often acted but is entirely without character, full of a pretty coquettish emotional display.

A long succession of other writers who attained to fame and honor as lyrists and epic poets were but seldom able to win success when they tried the stage; then it is to be ascribed to their poetic talents and only too often, in the first place, to their name. Otherwise they were entirely without influence in this field.

EMANUEL GEIBEL, the most popular lyrist of this period, wrote the tragedies, *König Roderich* (1842) and *Sophonisbe* (1868), also the pleasant comedy, *Meister Andrea* (1847), but only his *Brunhild* (1861) gained a certain popularity because the great figures of the

Nibelungen were toned down to correspond to the prevailing taste.

A similar fate in drama fell to the lot of PAUL HEYSE. In the long succession of his greater plays there are only two, *Hans Lange* (1866) and *Kolberg* (1868), which attained a fair popularity on the stage. Besides these perhaps *Die Göttin der Vernunft* (1870), *Don Juans Ende* (1883), *Die Weisheit Salomos* (1886) and *Maria von Magdala* (1899) are worthy of mention, the latter because of the political agitation called forth by the censorship. Closely connected with his main field, the short story, are his short dramas in one act, of which he has written a great number, all of them presenting clearly a tragic incident but without real dramatic qualities. Such are *Unter Brüdern, Ehrenschulden* and *Im Bunde der Dritte* (1886).

With a short comedy, *Durchs Ohr* (1865), WILHELM JORDAN, the author of *Die Nibelungen*, also obtained, at least once, recognition as a dramatist because of his charm and resonant rhymed-verse. Quite unsuccessful were the attempts of Friedrich Bodenstedt, Hermann Lingg, Count Adolf von Schack, Martin Greif, Robert Hamerling, Otto Roquette, Friedrich Spielhagen, and Felix Dahn, so that we can spare ourselves mention of any particular work.

SUMMARY

The general impression of German dramatic production and of the German stage during the fifty-five years
from 1830–85 is entirely unsatisfactory. All forceful
progressive movements seem to have died away; the old
worn-out fields are cultivated with ever-decreasing
profit, the petrified forms resist every attempt at improvement. The cultivation of formal beauty is the
highest aim. Morality is repressed in favor of conventional middle-class ethics. Everything reflecting the
spirit of the age is carefully avoided by upper-class
writers as dangerous and hostile to art while some op-
position-natures give vent to their hatred of existing
conditions by rude and formless contempt of law and
morals.

Middle-class drama both of the more serious and the
brighter kind loses the worthy character which class-
consciousness and the treatment of social differences had
formerly given it and aims only at providing entertainment. The fantastic style of the farce, the sound
humor of the folk-play, degenerate into nasty vulgarity
and stale puns. Actors lose serious ambition and all
desire to adapt themselves to their tasks. "Stars" mis-
use the great works of the classic writers as the sport of
their surprising tricks and destroy co-operation in acting. Care in rehearsals and in the external decoration
of the scenes, obedience to the directions of the author
and reverence for his creation are lost gradually and
entirely.

And yet the ideal drama had a more numerous and
more grateful public than ever before or since. The
longing for freedom grew intoxicated on the speeches of

Posa and Tell, the desire for a genuine free humanity
got satisfaction in Goethe's characters, and pity for all
oppressed and faith in an adjustment of all differences
in some higher state was satisfied in Lessing's *Nathan*
instead of in life. Schiller's popularity reached its
highest point in this period. The celebration of the
hundredth anniversary of his birth in 1859 was made
a brilliant festival in which all Germans took enthusiastic part, with the feeling that in his poetry the best
which filled their own souls had been uttered, the unful-
filled longing for the freedom, unity and greatness of
the Fatherland.

When a succession of mighty deeds of war and Bis-
marck's genius brought these thoughts and aspirations
down from the airy kingdom of ideals to the firm ground
of reality, then was lost to art and especially to the
drama, that last support which had kept it from sinking down completely into a cultivation of external form
and low epicureanism. Therefore the years from 1870–
80 became the saddest in the history of the modern German drama.

FRIEDRICH HEBBEL

From this background stands out the brilliant creative work of FRIEDRICH HEBBEL, the greatest dramatist
that Germany has produced since the days of the classic
writers. And he became such while struggling on with
heart of steel against the temporal needs of life and at
the same time striving to gain a settled philosophy of
the world and art, without any aid but his belief in
himself and his calling.

A descendant of a sturdy race of the "Dithmarsen,"

he saw the light of day March 18, 1813, at Wesselburen in Holstein in the cramped home of a bricklayer. His father, by nature a man of great talents, grew bitter in the unceasing struggle for the necessities of life, for "poverty had taken the place of his soul." All the mortifications which lowliness and need could cause a highminded spirit Friedrich Hebbel's early developed pride had to endure, but under the pressure his will-power grew and at the same time his thought and power of imagination expanded. From his fourteenth year he was in service as secretary to a narrow-minded man, the parish bailiff Mohr in Wesselburen. He soon grew intellectually far above his environment, working un-wearyingly at his education, reading and reflecting.

He, too, grew enthusiastic at first over the lofty diction of Schiller, then became enchanted with the shadowy figures which E. T. A. Hoffmann sketched with pecul-iarly realistic touches, and at last through Uhland's poem, *Des Sängers Fluch,* found the way to his own con-ception of art. Of these points he says in his diary: "I had up to this time felt very comfortable in my strumming in imitation of Schiller and had listened to and picked up many a doubt from the philosopher and many a rule for beauty from the æsthete. But now Uhland took me into the depths of a human heart and thereby into the depths of nature. I saw how he scorned nothing except what I had up to this time looked upon as the greatest thing—reflection. I saw that he understood how to find a spiritual bond between him-self and all things; that he, removed from all wilfulness and prejudice—I know no more significant word—knew how to trace everything back, even the wondrous and the mystical, to the simply human; how every one of his poems had its peculiar vital point and yet was only to be completely understood and estimated by looking back over the whole work of the poet. . . . Not without being close to despair, indeed to madness, did I gain this first result, that the poet must not write *into* nature but *out* from it. It is not to be estimated how far I was still removed from the conception of the first and only law of art, namely, to illustrate the infinite from the individual phenomenon."

Hebbel's villenage had lasted for eight years when the authoress, Amalie Schoppe, interested herself in him and made it possible for him to remove to Hamburg. Here he was now to supplement the defective education of his youth, but instead of this he wrote in his diary the thoughts which poured in upon him, his impressions of people and the results of his self-observation. At the head he set these words: "I am not beginning this notebook merely to please my future biographer, although with my prospects of immortality I can be certain that I will find one. It is to be the music-book of my heart and preserve the key notes, which my heart gives forth, faithfully and for my edification in future days."

The scanty aid of his patroness, who expected as thanks obedience to her narrow-minded advice, aimed only at quick bread-winning, was not of so much use to Hebbel as the devotion of the faithful Elise Lensing, for whom no sacrifice was too great, and who had recognised his greatness long before the world knew of him. He had indeed nothing to offer her but friendship and esteem and when later a deep and genuine love took possession of him, Elise had to give way. Hebbel was not ungrateful and not cruel but only clear and firm in thought and feeling in spite of all his gentleness of disposition. Hand in hand with Elise he could not have reached and maintained the height of his development.

His development was soon so far advanced that he considered it his life's work to symbolize his inner life as far as it was fixed in important instances in word and figure. This self-description meant at the same time something higher because art was to him *realized philosophy* as the world was *realized idea*. But he did not, like the Classicists and Romanticists, support himself by a fixed and final conception of the world which solves contradictions by an appeal to a higher unity. He declares the problematical to be the breath of life to poetry and its only source, that for it anything finished, perfect and dormant, is as little in existence as the healthy body for the physician.

Hebbel sees the deep plague spots of the day, he feels in himself the feverish ague which shakes diseased society, the conflicts, the contradictions of life for which there is no solution. The class of literature in which all this is artistically presented is for him, *tragedy*. It has to do with what is incurable and unavoidable in man's fate and, because he is so conscious of its office, he is zealous against unfruitful coquetting with the beautiful and against the one-sidedness of the drama, because it is either historical, social or philosophical. In his plays he joins all three divisions to make a new one which always, even when portraying the past, reflects the present and its struggles, and at the same time, from a lofty standpoint, lightens up the inner spirit of the times.

In Hebbel is found a cool, keen intellect, finding

satisfaction in a dialectic which is often subtle, a glowing sensuousness and a thorough conception of reality combined with a perfect comprehension of causes and a clear understanding of his own times, its problems and needs looked at from the point of view of universal history. He is not full of contradictions but of a grand many-sidedness, the consistency of which, however, cannot be perceived offhand. He lacks joy in the little charms of life, the quiet enjoyment of nature, the blind enthusiasm of youth or the beautiful and noble, but so much the deeper does he feel true greatness and with really dignified contempt does he score what is vulgar. His earlier works lack harmony, because he did not find it in himself and in the world and because he was too proud to be willing to delude himself and others by a delusion into overlooking what was painful and hateful. But this harmony is by no means equivalent to artistic perfection, as many suppose; if one considers that an artist is great because with the aid of great ability he brings a deep, inner content clearly to view, then Hebbel is to be counted among the great artists, although simplicity of feeling and production was denied him. Only too often does his discussion of problems cause neglect of the real purpose of the drama, viz: to present scenes full of life and characters that are humanly significant.

To his student years in Heidelberg and Munich, full of poverty and wretchedness, and only endurable because of Elise Lensing's aid, he owes less increase in knowledge than growth and maturity of heart and mind. Even at that time he was making great plans and in a poem written on a later visit to Munich, the following words occur:

Hier zeigte wie im Traume
Sich mir die Judith schon,
Dort unterm Tannenbaume
Sah ich den Tischlerssohn.
Da drüben winkte leise
Mir Genovevas Hand,
Und in des Weihers Kreise
Fand ich den Diamant.

When he returned to Hamburg in 1839, he wrote *Judith,* the first of the works referred to in the above lines. Just as clearly as Goethe's *Götz von Berlichingen* or Schiller's *Räuber* does this first drama of Hebbel's also bear the marks of exuberant power, too glaring colors, stormy revolt and feverish passion. But when we look into its contents we find nothing of youthful vagueness of thought or of artistic purpose and at the same time the author has the greatest and most unerring command of form.

Biblical subjects had in earlier days been long popular on the French and German stage. The Classicists and Romanticists had turned away from them because the field seemed to have been exhausted and individualism thought there was no place to be found for it there. At that time Gutzkow had just tried, in a drama *König Saul,* to treat a biblical incident in modern fashion and to justify it psychologically. But his power was not equal to the task and when Hebbel heard the play praised he set up his *Judith* as a contrast. In the biblical narrative belief in God, which is a living faith in Judith, triumphs over the heathen. Her woman's feelings are not considered in what she does, nor is Holofernes, her opponent, given features which surpass those typical of a conqueror and tyrant. Here Hebbel's art steps in to supplement. Holofernes becomes the mighty representative of unbroken personality, which, as a power with equal rights, boldly opposes, like the giants of old, the world-will, i. e., God. With his exaggerated feeling of power, the expression of which sometimes appears grotesque, Holofernes is just the right man to prove by his fall the greatness of God, and the victory of eternal law. The means which God employs is Judith. To become his instrument, she must possess qualities which make her stand out prominently from the multitude of women.

Judith is an Oriental woman of a strongly sensual nature, endowed with great spirit. Among her faint-hearted fellow-countrymen she did not find the man she longed for. She had been married, but her husband, early deceased, had, with inexplicable timidity, as if in the presence of something incomprehensible, not ventured to touch her. Now she is living shut up in her home as a virgin widow. She had plunged into the eternal One as one plunges into deep water, that is, she drowns the thoughts of her condition, which is an enigma to herself, in an unswerving faith in the secret will of God, until, through Holofernes, suffering comes upon the country and her own city is besieged. She hears that Holofernes kills women by kisses and embraces, just as he does men by spear and sword. Something whispers to her: "Had he known that you were within the walls of the city, he would have come for your sake alone." Judith answers with a sudden thought which betrays her desire to see and possess this man. "If that should be true then I should only need to go out to him and my city and land would be saved." But she is still far from this resolve. Only when the suffering of the city had become very

great and no aid was to be discovered, does she feel
certain that the invisible God had chosen her for his
instrument to save his people. And while driven out
into the hostile camp, as if by an inward force, she
believes she is fulfilling the will of the Highest, but
when she stands in the presence of Holofernes the
woman in her awakes; what was driving her out to him
was unconscious longing for the man himself. In vain
she prays: "God of my fathers, protect me from myself,
that I be not compelled to honor what I despise! He
is a man." She yields to him and when her desire
is satisfied, she becomes conscious that she has been
unfaithful to her mission. If she now slays Holofernes
she is no longer the instrument of God, but she is
avenging on him her own desire which she recognises
as sin. A selfish wish instead of religious enthusiasm
and patriotism had led her into his arms and not with
rejoicing, as in the biblical report, but as a broken
sinner she goes back to her people, trembling with the
fear that she will bear Holofernes a son who will immor-
talize her crime. But Jehovah is the victor. He has
broken the mightiest of men: he has also destroyed the
woman who was this instrument. His power alone
remains undiminished, shown to be stronger than ever.

Somewhat subtle is Hebbel's motivation of Judith's
deed because of her peculiar condition of being neither
wife nor maiden. At the same time her relation to
Holofernes is to represent the never-ending conflict of
the sexes and the metaphysical basis of this relation.
Both figures in common embody the nature of the strong-
willed poet with passionate desires. The social instincts
serve as a background and stand out strikingly, as never

before on the German stage, in the powerful folk-scenes of the third act.

Everywhere Hebbel's chief aim is that which he recognised as the most important in Shakespeare's art, "to disclose the roots of morality in life in the grandest possible manner by cutting away the weeds that cover them up." Nowhere is it his object in his works to plead the cause of an abstract idea. He is an absolute Realist although the form keeps clear of all trivial reproduction of reality and his language indulges in bold metaphors. *Judith* may be called the first modern drama of the nineteenth century because here for the first time, unconcerned about artistic tradition, the expression of the peculiar nature of the present is attempted in a suitable corresponding dramatic style.

It was put upon the stage in Berlin, July 6, 1840, a bold venture, and at one stroke Hebbel became known. The critics, with all their objections, had after all to acknowledge the depth of thought, the loftiness of artistic purpose and the astonishing maturity of the young author.

After a somewhat lengthy pause a work, which had been planned earlier, was finished, *Genoveva* (1840–1841). Once more he chose an old, well-known subject which he tried to explain by human motives. For a long time he had been thinking over the problem which for him consisted in this, that a noble, yielding, innocent, youthful nature because of sensual love to a transfigured saint falls a victim to criminal madness. That is the misfortune, the guilt and the justification of Golo, the real hero of this tragedy. Genoveva, on the other hand, steps into the background and remains inwardly unaffected by all that befalls her. The most guilty is the husband who believes in her infidelity upon mere circumstantial evidence, because according to Hebbel it is far more sinful not to suspect the divine in our neighborhood, and without further investigation to take it for its black adversary, than to demolish it in world-destroying madness because we can not possess it.

In spite of the fact that Hebbel's work is superior by far in genuine poetic merit to the works of the same name by Maler Müller and Ludwig Tieck (*vide* p. 10) yet he could not after all remove the fundamental weakness which lay in the legend, the preponderance of the epic and lyric, although he did with firm hand strengthen the plot in the earlier acts. In his work, too, the miraculous and the reflective gain too great an influence, and again the manner of treatment and the motivation of the chief characters is too subtle. Hebbel could not use the reconciliation which comes at the close of the old legend if he was to be true to his belief in the incurable nature of the world's woe. And yet to comply with the demand for it he wrote an epilogue in 1851, in which the forgiveness of all wrongdoing is brought about by the husband voluntarily offering to take upon himself all Genoveva's sufferings due to him, and by Genoveva forgiving Golo, her accuser, in the words of the Lord's Prayer. In the unhappy Golo Hebbel has revealed his own thoughts in the period of their development and in their antitheses; in this character therefore is the best key to an acquaintance with the young poet.

The whole drama reveals his view of the world with the same power and with still stronger proofs than

Judith. Everything that happens is only from our standpoint good or bad, everything originates with the world-will which rests in God and the business of the poet is to reproduce in his work of art, in a clear and comprehensible manner, the working of this will back of life which represents it veiled and unconsciously. In order to be able to do this he must dive down deep in the abyss of personality to discover the first motives for the acts, which have their root in the soil of the eternal interdependence of all things. In this connection *Genoveva* with all its dramatic faults is very significant.

In the prologue to the comedy, *Der Diamant,* which was finished immediately after *Genoveva* (1841), it is said by the poet:

> Er ist in die bewegte Welt
> Als fester Mittelpunkt gestellt,
> Der, unberührt von Ebb' und Flut,
> In sich gesättigt, schweigend ruht,
> Weil er in sich jedweden Kreis
> Begonnen und beschlossen weiss,
> Und weil in ihm der Urgeist still
> Die Perl', sein Abbild, zeugen will,
> Das, wenn es in die Zeitlichkeit
> Hinaustritt, jeden Riss der Zeit,
> Schon dadurch heilt, dass sie erkennt,
> Was sie vom ew'gen Wesen trennt.

His purpose to give, in a cheerful light, a picture of the working of the original spirit did not, however, succeed. Here, too, it was not a question with Hebbel of individual phenomena but of the connection of trifling, seemingly unimportant and ridiculous incidents with the eternal conditions of existence. Through the diamond is to be revealed the innermost nature of all who struggle for its possession. But especially the scenes which take place at a fanciful court are lifeless and contrast too strongly with the rough comic of the rest, the nature of which corresponds to the highest conception of what is comical and yet is not easily and directly comprehensible.

When Hebbel sought aid in Kopenhagen from the King of Denmark, his sovereign, a handsome travelling scholarship was granted him for two years. Even before he left his home-land the greater portion of that tragedy had been written which of all his works was best to reflect national character, *Maria Magdalena.* It was finally finished in Paris and appeared in 1844 with its important preface on the relation of dramatic art to the times. It is based on incidents which Hebbel saw in Munich when he was living with a cabinet-maker who, like his hero, was called Anton. "I saw how all the members of this worthy middle-class family grew gloomy when the gendarmes led away the foolish son. I was deeply moved when I saw the daughter, who waited upon me, really breathe freely again when I joked and fooled with her in the old fashion." Hebbel had become the *confidant* of this daughter; from her confessions Clara's story took its origin. The fate of the unhappy, deserted sweetheart had often been made use of for dramatic effect even before Goethe wrote his Gretchen-tragedy, but mostly from the standpoint that the seducer belonged to the nobility, the fallen girl of the middle classes, and that fear of a rough honorable father drove her to child-murder or to suicide. The difference in rank does not exist in Hebbel's play. It is no longer the oppressed citizen of the eighteenth century but the middle-class of the

nineteenth which esteems itself the real representative
of the people. But only so much the narrower is the
constraint of life which destroys all free judgment
and all free conduct because their social position and
self-respect is based upon traditional ideas of honor
and right and not upon a view of morals arrived at
independently. Hebbel had already written in his
diary at Munich: "There is no worse tyrant than the
common man in his family circle." He had learned
that in his own youth, so many of the impressions
of which had gone into the *Maria Magdalena,* and he
now copied it with its most striking characteristics into
the figure of the cabinet-maker Anton. In this drama
everything is unconditional necessity. The character
of the people is entirely conditioned by the class to
which they belong; for them this means fate, and the
ethical point of view peculiar to this class suffers no
opposition from any individual. No one is capable of
venturing an independent judgment of the world that
closes him in; it decides as to fortune and misfortune,
life and death, and from this comes the depressing
feeling left by this great work of art.

It is not a question here of a struggle between equal
opponents, but the whole of middle-class society goes
to smash from within before the eyes of the spectators
without any new or better substitute showing itself
in the background. To uphold middle-class respectability at all costs is the main point just as in the older
middle-class drama, but while this latter shows only
the advantageous exterior of a society supported by
firm principles, Hebbel lights up the interior and proves
how much that is humanly valuable is destroyed for
the sake of appearance and how rotten the pillars of

this society really are. The unfortunate Clara, who was originally to give the name to the play, is a victim of the class whose views mean for her the eternal cosmic system. When she believes herself deserted by the lover of her youth she becomes the loveless betrothed of Treasurer Leonhard merely to escape derision and to stifle in her own heart her love for the supposedly faithless one. Her lover returns and keeps away from her because of her engagement. She yields herself to her betrothed because he demands this proof of her affection and, according to the views of their class, this cannot be considered a grievous sin with engaged couples. "If she is going to become my wife then she knows that she is risking nothing." Then all is suddenly changed because of a supposed theft by her brother, which covers Clara's family with shame and causes the loss of her small dowry. The Treasurer cancels the engagement, especially when an advantageous union with the ugly niece of the mayor offers itself and Clara's prayers cannot bring him back to her. Even the lover is completely steeped in class-prejudice and says when he hears of Clara's trouble: "Nobody can get over that! To be obliged to lower her eyes in the presence of the fellow in whose face one would like to spit? . . . Or one would have to put the dog who knows it out of the way by shooting!" Clara had sworn to the father that she would not bring disgrace upon him and therefore goes voluntarily to death. But even this sacrifice is made in vain, for her purpose of avoiding the suspicion of suicide is unsuccessful. Thus everything works together to destroy her and the father whose sole life-purpose is the preservation of a stainless reputation. In the closing words of Master Anton, "Ich verstehe die Welt nicht mehr," middle-class ethical standards proclaim their bankruptcy; they fall in ruins before our eyes.

With *Maria Magdalena* begins the social drama of the present day. No longer is the contrast of classes brought before us in passionate conflicts but society is described and its defects revealed. Therefore the delineation of conditions becomes more important than the plot and a new technique is the result. Only the last stages of a course of destiny are shown; these are just as much settled by general conditions as by the peculiarities of the people concerned and from this the necessity of all preceding incidents is analytically deduced.

The principal difficulty with this technique consists in making known without omissions the necessary assumptions in the course of the plot and yet dovetailing them without effort into the dialogue in such a way that the interest of the spectators is retained to the close and the action advances continuously. Because of these peculiar conditions, the modern society-drama is akin to Greek tragedy in its construction and in its portrayal of typical characters but with the reservation that, conformably to the complicated conditions of the present, the personages are no such simple creations as those which the Greek writers present. The general impression derived from both classes is one of fate. But while in the Greek the justice of the course of the world is proven, here the final result is a depressing conviction of the unconditional and unfailing effect of social and natural laws by which freedom of action seems done away with.

The representatives of "Young Germany" had already

aimed at such a drama theoretically. Hebbel came independently to similar requirements, supported far more strongly by thought and experience. He satisfied them in his *Maria Magdalena* more completely than his predecessors and with the same devices as his most important successor, Ibsen. In the society-dramas of his middle period the latter stands entirely on the shoulders of Hebbel.

Thus *Maria Magdalena* is the cornerstone of the new dramatic art but at the same time in another respect the conclusion of the old. In the magnificent figure of Master Anton, hewn as it were from granite, we see the descendant of music-master Miller in Schiller's *Kabale und Liebe*. He lacks, however, the joyful self-confidence, the fighting spirit and the rude cheeriness of his ancestors. The quills, which the middle-class citizen in the early days of that class wore on the outside, have been turned inwards; he does not venture to struggle, he thinks nothing at all about people, nothing bad, nothing good, and only in his sense of middle-class honor does he see the standard which he applies to all things. With his great heroic spirit he is held fast in a narrow circle of thought and clings to the belief that the existing cosmic order is just and complete. If this belief goes to pieces, then he too, and his class, must be ruined. That is proven in the younger generation which grows up beside him light-hearted and assertive.

To him who looks deeper there are revealed in *Maria Magdalena* the causes of the convulsions which society has witnessed since 1840, except that here that influence is not yet visible which was gained soon afterwards by the new social forces which came into being because of the development of industry. No longer the upper classes, but the organised masses of workmen, demanding equality, are now the opponents with which the middle classes have to contend. The outlook opens upon a new middle-class drama which now does not picture a condition of rest but the passionate struggles of two mighty opponents. To find for this just as complete an expression on the stage as *Maria Magdalena* gives of the self-destruction of the middle class is reserved as one of the greatest artistic problems for the twentieth century.

Hebbel's criticism of society is continued in the two dramatic works which had their source in his impressions of travel. In Paris he took delight in the larger bustling life going on all around him. He had, it is true, been born and had grown up in a small place but was by nature and inclination a metropolitan who would feel permanently comfortable only in the full stream of busy public life. Then when he went to Rome, the ruins which formerly had spoken so eloquent a language to Goethe could only speak to him of vanished greatness. The deep moral degradation and the wretched government of the city, as well as in the neighboring kingdom of Naples, where he stayed later, confirmed his view of the incurable nature of the world's conditions and again he sought to give pictures of the present, in which they should be delineated.

In November, 1845, he found a second home in Vienna, where he had been detained by an accident. It was a year later before there stirred in him again the impulse to create and he wrote the two dramas of the present, whose scene of action is laid in Italy; the tragi-comedy, *Ein Trauerspiel in Sizilien*, and the trag-

edy, *Julia*. Both are taken from the sphere of the
disgusting, of the simply horrible which Hebbel thinks
is the result of modern conditions. In the first the
fundamental element of humor is to so combine the horrible with the bizarre that the one as well as the
other will only have a moderated effect. The fearful
appears in the lowest form because in the play the
obsolete police-governed state is fate, and at the same
time the contrasts of economic inequality represent the
fearful danger of an unevenly increasing wealth. The
effect of this mixture of the horrible and the comic
can not but be disagreeable.

The very same is true of *Julia*, which likewise is
intended to reflect Italian conditions before 1848. The
heroine finds herself in the same condition as Clara in
Hebbel's middle-class tragedy; her father, like Master
Anton, considers himself a just man but the solution
of the problem is complicated because other factors
play a part. The note of responsibility to the coming
generation is already struck in the play when Count
Bertram, shattered in health by excesses, declares that
marriage between "life" and "death," between healthy
youth and worn-out debility, is the "mother of ghosts."
Thus there sounds in our ears not only the subject but
even, accidentally, the title of one of the most significant of Ibsen's works.

Artistic command of his material, clearness and certainty in grasping reality here fail the author and
therefore, in spite of the historic importance which
Julia plainly possesses, in spite of the scenes of inimitable grandeur and beauty, justly praised by Otto Ludwig, the work after all must likewise be considered
a failure.

The bitter despair voiced in it is an echo of Hebbel's youth. When he wrote the *Trauerspiel in Sizilien* and *Julia* (1846) the pressure of poverty had been taken from him, he had found in Vienna a second home, and in the noble actress Christine Enghaus a life companion such as he needed. No unconquerable passion had led him to her because, as he said, the whole man in him belonged to poetry, to that power which to him was the most important, for out of it alone springs his own happiness and the advantage which the world can derive from him.

What new works he wrote from now on were not to embody eternal contrasts in that accidental form which the circumstances of his own time gave them. He chose by preference the turning-points of history where these contrasts, represented by two ages and their points of view, had come together in mightiest collision. This was the origin of the great works of his last period, at their head *Herodes und Mariamne* (1847–48). Herod, whom fate has placed at that point of historic development where the heathen-Jewish and the dawning Christian world are both visible at the same time, sees in his wife, in agreement with the old passing view-point, merely a costly possession; she, however, loves him with a different, to him new and incomprehensible love, which seeks its happiness in sacrifice. This is the source of the conflict in this thoughtful drama and it is made greater by the general conditions of the time and by those peculiar to the Jewish tetrarch dependent upon Rome. In him pulses in feverish excitement the blood of his great forefathers and upon him weighs the curse of the old egoistic ethics and of the heart-loneliness springing therefrom. *He-*

rodes und Mariamne became a universal drama in the
highest sense. Hebbel did not aim at describing
"Jealousy, monster of frightful mien," as Calderon had
done before with the same subject; on the contrary,
his very successful purpose was to make the historic
anecdote the expression of necessary human conduct.
Mariamne is beheaded, but that which was in her lives
on and, when Herod immediately afterwards gives command for the murder at Bethlehem in order to destroy
the Messiah of this new world, his blind rage cannot
stay its victory.

In this tragedy Hebbel has clearly striven for that
pure beauty of form which graces the works of Schiller
and Goethe, but he does so without giving up anything
of his own peculiar nature. He now dispenses with any
display of mere force, any subtle dialectic, any emphasis
upon what is striking and strange in the characters
and if apparently anything of the kind is still left in
them, then the impression arises only from the fact
that Hebbel penetrates deeper than earlier dramatists
into the mysterious origin of personality and discovers
features there which at first sight strike one as irregular
and wilful.

Full of great significance are also the two dramas,
seemingly dashed off with easy touch, *Der Rubin* (1849)
and *Michel Angelo* (1850). *Der Rubin* conceals under
the cloak of an Eastern fairy-story so much deep
thought that it can scarcely be interpreted fully and,
especially to the superficial Viennese public, was just as
little comprehensible as Grillparzer's kindred comedy,
Weh' dem, der lügt. The rights of the more highly
gifted as compared with the mass and the excuse for the
assumptions of the lesser sort is the subject of *Michel*

Angelo. The play is an artist's merry anecdote "of cerulean hue" which with the greatest sense of justice does not deny self-consciousness, and is indispensable for the full understanding of Hebbel, however little its merit as a work of art may be in comparison with his other plays.

Hebbel has also accepted the right of the whole, as contrasted with the individual, as existing unconditionally for the freest of the sons of earth, the artist. He defined more generally the value of eminent people in the most beautiful of his tragedies, *Agnes Bernauer* (1851), in which beauty in itself means tragedy. Agnes Bernauer's beauty is in a way a privilege which the individual assumes over against the whole; it kindles the most violent passions and in its innocency causes greater harm than the blackest sinner can accomplish.

Hebbel himself has thus characterized the idea of this drama: "In it is expressed quite simply the relation of the individual to society. Accordingly it is illustrated by two characters, of whom the one belongs to the highest classes and the others to the lowest, that the individual, however grand and great, noble and beautiful he may be, must yield to society under all circumstances, because in it and in its necessary formal expression, the state, all human natures lives, in the individual, however, only the single phase comes to development. That is the stern bitter lesson for which I expect no thanks from the shallow democracy of our times, but it runs through all history and whoever cares to study my earlier dramas in their sum total, instead of conveniently stopping with individual ones, will find that it has already been proclaimed even there as far as each separate sphere permitted."

As in the case of the other subjects which had already been treated before Hebbel's time, he is in these also completely distinguished from his predecessors by his point of view, not because of a striving after originality but because he knows how to go deeper into the nature of things.

All former writers had glorified Agnes Bernauer, the unfortunate and beautiful barber's daughter of Augsburg, as a martyr, and pictured her murder as an act of revenge, of patriotism or of cruel class-pride. Hebbel proves the necessity of her death for the sake of higher interests. He shows that Duke Ernest, who has her killed, sacrifices his feelings as a man for the good of the state and that the tragic note of heroic renunciation is inherent in his genuine greatness. He shows further that the son who puts the possession of the sweetheart above everything else must first be trained for the ruler's office to which he is born. Similarly Agnes' death means for her husband the victory of the sense of duty over selfish, sensual desires, as does the death of the *Jüdin von Toledo* for the king in Grillparzer's drama. Agnes falls a victim, without protection and without a struggle, and her death, which does not mark the close but the central point of the tragedy, cannot impair the great and uplifting effect of the whole. In this *Agnes Bernauer* is most clearly distinguished from *Maria Magdalena,* which stands next to it in other respects because of its well-knit, compact construction, its wealth of individual features and the compelling logic of the motivation. The language is smoother than in the early work, and happily colored by the slightly archaic touch of the time of the action.

For the comprehension of a woman's feelings in their

deepest depths Agnes is as little adapted as any of
Hebbel's earlier woman-characters, because in them all
special conditions of personality permit what is generally legitimate for their sex only to shine as it were
through a mist. *Gyges und sein Ring* (1854) delineates
a woman who, completely cut off from the world, without any disturbing influence from outside, develops one-
sidedly in the specifically female direction. Her exaggerated feeling of modesty feels even the glance of
a stranger as a stain which she must remove at all
costs. Perhaps purity is here exaggerated to a paradox
but everything develops logically from this feeling which
has complete mastery over Rhodope. She says to herself: "Only my husband may see my face; therefore
he who has seen it must become my husband and therefore must first murder my earlier husband. But I
cannot possibly live in marriage bonds with the murderer," and she stabs herself before the altar after
the outrage to her feeling of purity is atoned for by
her marriage with Gyges. Kandaules, the husband, is
not merely a boaster as in the legend told by Herod-
otus. Hebbel deduces his conduct from the deepest
motives of his nature. As the descendant of a great
family, as the last of the Heraclides he aims at intro-
ducing a new era for his people. He lacks reverence
for traditional custom, for the historical as well as the
enlightened, the liberal. He depreciates the old values
without being able to put new ones in their place.

Hebbel thought that he had here found the point
of intersection in which the ancient and the modern
atmosphere pass over into one another. He supposed
he had solved in a general human fashion, comprehensible for all times, a problem such as could only have

originated in that legendary period. He did not intend
to give the drama any particular idea as a background
but to his greatest surprise, after its completion, there
suddenly issues out of it, like an island out of the
ocean, the idea of custom as that which conditions and
binds everything together.

In this in reality lies an aid to the full understanding of the strange work. We find another in the comparison of Rhodope with the figure of Nora, seemingly
so very different from her, in Ibsen's *Doll's House,*
of whom one is already reminded by Hebbel's *Mariamne*. Here as there the slumbering, dreamy soul of a
wife who accepts life as something to be taken for
granted wakes up to independent activity and experience. Here as there the husband believes that in her
he has a possession with which he may do as he likes
and has to make grievous atonement for his error. In
both dramas the right of the wife to respect for her
peculiar nature is maintained and finally gains the
victory. But while with Ibsen all lines come out sharply
in the clear cold light of reality, Hebbel envelops his
figures in the faint light of the mystical. Gyges' ring,
which is superfluous for the real purpose of the author,
fulfils the object of awakening the feeling of the mysterious associations of nature, of the riddle in its phenomena which is not to be solved by reason. Hebbel
thought of putting the drama on the French stage and
certainly he was right in his statement that in outward
form it was as nearly related to Racine as it was in
essence different. For just as in the great French
tragedy writer, so here there is united with strict forms
borrowed from the classical writers, a sympathetic, thoroughly modern sentiment and a deep subjectivity.

There is hardly a modern work so near in form as this
to the ideal of classic art and to the noble simplicity
and modest grandeur of the ancients.

No one but a writer with full strength in himself
and with a complete mastery of all the resources of his
art could succeed in such a work. Hebbel's helpful
home-life, the recognition of his work by a few, but
these the best, his own feeling of maturity permit him
now to look above him with the greatest gratitude. In
a prayer he calls out:

" Götter, öffnet die Hände nicht mehr, ich würde erschrecken,
Denn ihr gabt mir genug; hebt sie nur schirmend empor! "

And now he collected his whole strength for a drama
in which he aimed at placing on the stage before
the eyes of his nation *Die Nibelungen,* the greatest
figures in German legend. Before him Fouqué and
Raupach had contended for this prize, and Richard
Wagner's great work, *Die Nibelungen,* had just been
written. Modestly Hebbel limited his purpose to making the dramatic contents of the old epic soluble. But,
in spite of the fact that he did not intend to explore
its poetic-mythical contents, he could not, true to his
whole nature, cut out the mythical altogether. Seven
years, from 1855 to 1862 he worked, often interrupted
indeed, on the play, and the result was a trilogy of
eleven acts.

Hebbel dispensed with the mysterious expedients of
the northern legend, Siegfried's double marriage and
the potion producing loss of memory, because according
to his scarcely tenable view they would have expected
too much of a modern public and he therefore allowed
the characters to act in full freedom. He took the

bas-reliefs of the old poem down from the wall and
traced what was monstrous back to the universal-human
without touching the heart of the legend, because he
felt himself here the interpreter of something higher.
He says: "One must, with such a subject, drop out
nine-tenths of the culture and yet manage with the
rest without becoming dry. That I have practised self-
denial, all just critics will sooner or later acknowledge;
I aimed merely at bringing this great national epic
dramatically nearer to the public without any additions
of my own."

One need only compare Geibel's *Brunhild,* which appeared during the writing of Hebbel's drama, with the
latter in order to recognize that every attempt to bring
the incidents, the characters and the spirit of the
Nibelungenlied near to modern feeling takes from the
subject its grandeur and its peculiar character. In
Geibel's work Brunhild becomes a coquettish woman
taking vengeance for despised love; with Hebbel she
appears giantlike in her emotions; she and Siegfried
are the last of a dying race.

Once more, as is so often the case in Hebbel, we stand
at the turning-point of two periods. In Hagen the old
is represented with its unyielding nature, its lack of
higher morality, its untamed hate and jealousy. Even
fidelity is counted to him as guilt. The Nibelungs must
perish because their perjury over Siegfried's dead body
has shown them all to be men blinded and entangled
in narrow selfishness. Kriemhild belongs to the new
period with her quiet gentleness but withers away in
heart; world-weary and in despair she has to do duty
as an avenger. At the close Dietrich von Bern embodies the new epoch of Christianity, heroically but

humbly, even when the crowns of the world are placed in his hands.

Even Hebbel's mighty talent did not succeed in overcoming the epic character of the Nibelungen-theme. In his work, too, what happens outweighs the inner changes finding expression in action, although the mighty collision of opposites at the climaxes and the wonderful depth of characterization just at these points produce the appearance of the dramatic. If *Die Nibelungen,* of all the works of Hebbel after the *Maria Magdalena,* at present appear most frequently on the stage and receive the greatest applause, they owe this to the national subject and to the lucidity of the characterization which is interspersed and overlaid with dialectical discussion of difficult problems, as happened so often in the earlier dramas of the author.

Hebbel seized upon a genuinely dramatic theme which had already attracted a number of poets, among them Schiller, in the *Demetrius* (1855–63), but death took the pen out of his hand also, Dec. 13, 1863, before the work was completed. At first he had been moved, like so many others, to supplement Schiller's fragment. At that time there was widely known only the sketch of a continuation, useless for the stage, which Körner had put together from Schiller's numerous and very divergent posthumous plans. But even leaving that out of the question, Hebbel's entirely different nature would have made it impossible for him to continue in Schiller's spirit and he soon came to the conviction that one could just as little begin to write on from where Schiller had left off, as begin to love from where another had ceased. Besides he wrongly supposed, misled by Körner's intimations, that Schiller had intended to

make his hero, as a conscious deceiver, fight in the last
acts to preserve his usurped throne, which was not the
case. He therefore sketched his own independent
framework, made his hero appear at first in lowliness,
as Schiller had done in the original plan of his first
act, and mixed into this portrait the feelings of his own
hard experience in youth. His Demetrius is destroyed
at the moment that he recognizes the unrighteousness
of his claim to the crown and after that thinks only
of the rescue of the friends who have given him their
aid. He is destroyed because he is too noble and pure
for the calling of a usurper which fate forces upon
him. But this solution carries with it the danger that
the hero will fall a victim to fate without resistance and
hence a depressing sense of the ruin of a pure innocent
nature takes the place of mighty tragedy. It must be
remembered that Hebbel had already described similar
fates in Genoveva, Maria Magdalena, Agnes Bernauer,
and Rhodope, but there had been placed beside them
such characters as Golo, Meister Anton, Duke Ernest,
and Kandaules, whose passionate energy had balanced
the lack of force in the female characters. Moreover,
these victims of fate were all women, whose sex in itself
makes one more easily forget the lack of energetic opposition.

Alongside the completed works of Hebbel there tower
aloft in his workshop, like mighty but only roughly chis-
elled granite blocks, a number of uncompleted dramatic
modellings of legendary and historic incidents. From
the years of his youth, before *Judith,* comes *Mirandola,* a
preliminary study for *Genoveva,* influenced, just as was
Der Vatermord (1831), by the popular tendencies of
the robber and fate drama prevalent at that time. In

Munich a succession of great historic personages appear to his vision: Julian the Apostate, the Maid of Orleans, Napoleon, figures from whom much passed over to Holofernes, Judith and Herod. Further Alexander the Great, his heart torn with doubt whether he was the son of Philip or Jupiter Ammon; then for a long time vacillating between drama and novel, the plan of *Die Ditmarschen,* the picture of the author's own countrymen with their defiant love of freedom, which was so brilliantly shown in the battle of Hemmingstedt against the Danes.

The greatest of these plans was that of *Moloch,* which from 1837 to Hebbel's death exercised its attractive power over him and yet, after repeated attempts, was not put into shape. It was certainly the loftiest idea of all that arose in the poet's mind but just for that reason offered the greatest difficulties to realization in form. In it he wished to illustrate the evolution of the religious and political relations which continue throughout the whole course of history, although modified considerably during the centuries. Rome, Carthage, and primitive German conditions were to form the background, the theme was the coming of culture to the barbarian. By Hiram, a fugitive from Carthage when destroyed by the Romans, the belief in Moloch, a mass of iron which he brought with him, is utilized to teach the barbarians the use of the bodily and intellectual powers, to make them recognize the value of culture and to form them into instruments of his revenge by awakening in them the longing for Italy. But their blind idolatrous belief in Moloch grows to an inward power which Hiram himself must recognize and to which he falls a victim. Thus there is presented in its beginnings the idea of God, growing out of an awe-filled worship of the unknown into the mightiest factor of the life of the soul.

The further stages in the evolution of mankind down to the present are the chief subject of Hebbel's completed dramas and his far more numerous plans. This is the case, for instance, with the great fragment, *Die Schauspielerin* (1848–1850). A woman aims at avenging herself on the whole race because the man whom she used to love is unworthy of her. She becomes an actress in order that through the characters in drama she may awaken love without responding to it. But a new passion for a second man enters her heart. The latter is willing to risk his life for her in a duel with the unworthy one, but because of anxiety for her lover, she now no longer charges the sex with the offences which the individual had committed. In Eugenia, the actress, the free woman with her rights and her feelings carries her point; she feels the stain upon her soul more than the sin against the body; she demands for herself the right of untrammeled decision over her fate, consideration equal to that for a man.

This appears to be an attempt to solve one of the chief questions of the day but appearances deceive. The rivalry of the sexes is not made to end but is transferred to another and nobler sphere.

In his fantastic sketch of the future, *Zu irgend einer Zeit* (1843–1848), Hebbel has also tried to throw a light out into the distant darkness. The satiric picture shows mankind sunk back again, because of communism, into the animal stage in which all individualism has vanished and blind necessity alone prevails.

Even in these beginnings which scarcely give hope

of a satisfactory artistic development, there is still shown, from all points of view, that which distinguishes Hebbel from the great mass of writers of his time, viz: the endeavor to startle and enrich men's hearts by the treatment of the deepest problems of life and society, but not to favor the worship of mere beauty or to satisfy the call for passionate experience by the old, threadbare conflicts and their conventional solutions.

So long as the great mass of spectators wish to see only such requirements fulfilled in serious drama, Hebbel cannot be their poet in spite of the fact that he does not really lack dramatic life and sensuous wealth of delineation. He himself has convincingly explained in numerous critical essays his aim and its justification, especially in the three long articles, *Mein Wort über das Drama* (1843), *Vorwort zu Maria Magdalena* (1844) and *Über den Stil des Dramas* (1847). Even during his life he had enthusiastic admirers and their number is still constantly growing, but general recognition of Hebbel as the greatest dramatist since Schiller has not yet resulted and it can only be hoped that it will come at no very distant time. The hindrances to this lie in his pessimism, in his preference for the abnormal rather than what is generally accepted, in his mingling of sensuous warmth and cold dialectic discussion, and in his clothing of modern problems in historical dress. These are easier to overcome, however, than the obscurity of his psychological hypotheses, the threads of which can often be followed only with difficulty. But just on this point the greatest of his successors, Ibsen, has broken down the earlier passive resistance and therefore the difficulties in the way of the complete understanding of Hebbel are to-day no longer so great as in his lifetime when he stood almost alone on the stage.

OTTO LUDWIG

The only writer who might have taken his place beside Hebbel, because of his endeavor to produce dramas in keeping with the spirit of the times and of real weight because of their contents and artistic merit, was OTTO LUDWIG, who was born at Eisfeld in Thuringia, Feb. 11, 1813, and died after a long and severe illness in Dresden, Feb. 25, 1865. But his lack of energetic, connected and unswerving effort towards the goal of artistic creation, his wrestling with technical problems and his uncertainty of judgment in regard to his own performances, made it impossible for him to stamp his own artistic personality upon any large number of great works. He said, ''The beautiful is never completed, it could always become still more beautiful.''

By ceaseless brooding he destroyed his own power of production and it was because of despair that he finally clung to Shakespeare as the dramatist who is in every way an absolute standard. Therefore it is with a certain sense of justice that all his posthumous discussions of dramatic creation are entitled *Shakespeare-Studien*, although they by no means have reference to Shakespeare alone.

In many respects he is nearly related to Hebbel; in his rejection of the classical drama of beauty, because ''everything is beautiful, nothing is ugly if it is only in its right place,'' in his demand for subjects suited to the times, in the reconciliation of art and life, and in his perception that the history of the tragic reveals itself as the history of the ethical interpretation of soul-conflicts. But he rejects the problem-drama entirely and would ask from poetry not to be made to think but to feel. In the influences of philosophy and of antiquity he sees the causes which led Schiller and his successors from the right path. He says: "Out of the confusion into which we have fallen because of reflection, reflection alone can bring us. We must through it rid ourselves of it." The great German authors had set themselves another problem than the dramatic. To them the drama was only a means and it had to make atonement therefor. Now it is a question of finding the way back to the drama, of recognising the dramatic duty of the times, and this he sees in the suppression of the lyrical and idyllic and in the reproduction of the great passions and of manly energy. From the reciprocal relations of the author, the actor and the public, the essential factors of the drama, he desires to develop his technique. He comes to the conclusion that the drama must come down to the common needs of the people who, as Ludwig says, attend the theatre to obtain a rest, not from the worries of life but from life itself. The dramatist is to bring something to everybody. While he is continually transposing the sum of human powers into a living play—these different requirements proceed essentially from the one-sided prominence usually attached to one of them—he restores again in the individual spectator, at least for the brief period of the full power of his magic, the original totality of the person, however much his particular position in life, his education or his experience of special daily professional work have put him out of joint and by developing to the greatest possible degree some parts of his being have left the others to waste away from lack of use.

In the dramatist Otto Ludwig the strongest impulse is that to truth, to a perfect and faithful representation of reality. How near he came to this goal is shown by his first acted drama, *Der Erbförster* (1845–1849). Like all Ludwig's works, this grew slowly and with great difficulty, out of a multitude of schemes. His own dramatic requirements give at the same time the essence of the play: "The motives follow one another quickly and urgently. There is to be no trace of effeminacy, one figure must always be stronger than the second, but none quixotic. The language must be pithy, popular, clear, robust, abounding in proverbs, in short, like Luther's. The rustling woods must always look down upon the scene. Reality must be made beautiful but not too restricted." But where Ludwig further requires that the play must "grow without cessation, seem to have root in Iffland and with its crown touch Shakespeare, and everything be simple, nothing either in character or in situation, affected or curious," then he was not able to satisfy his own demand.

Chief forester Christian Ulrich is a character much like Hebbel's Master Anton. Just as the latter is narrowed in his thought by class-consciousness and the ideas of right and honor peculiar to the lower classes, so, for the former, reality and its conditions vanish behind the thick green trees of the forest with which his life is bound up. While he believes he is upholding his rights he commits not only a series of grievous irregularities, but his clear eye also loses the power of sharp discernment and thereby he becomes the victim of unfortunate accidents which make him a criminal, the murderer of his daughter. But fate does not govern in this play as in Werner and Müllner, where an unfortunate coincidence of trifling circumstances brings about the painful result, but, on the other hand, these incidents become of significance only because feelings irritated to the highest degree destroy reflection and drive a man previously calm to act rashly and in wild sudden passion. Shakespeare's Othello is obviously the model for such a development. As in it, so in the *Erbförster*, the monstrous delusion which destroys the hero is the real subject of the drama and it keeps growing until it finally overpowers him.

This great drama has all the greater effect because the outward forms of middle-class tragedy are employed, which very rarely give room for the mighty passion that produces the highest tragic emotions and because the characters appear unpretentious and true to nature in language and gesture and without any pathos whatever. Ludwig did not indeed master the difficulty of making clear and convincing within this limitation the course of a mighty fate: the pettiness of the motives in the last acts makes the spectator misjudge the great purpose of the dramatist and the action in its second part seems to owe its impelling force more to something from without than from within. But even this fault is, from Ludwig's standpoint, of lesser importance because he aimed, as we have seen, at awakening a certain feeling; all else to him was only a means to that end and he required that he who wished to decide of the nature of the work must think of the impression and not of the means.

From the nature of the mountains and their inhabitants, the seclusion of the forester's house and the environment, comes the strangely mingled effect of *Der Erbförster*: fresh, spicy, chest-expanding forest air, free and beautiful nature, and in the people stupid narrowness, ineffectual desire and petty performance.

The first two factors of the drama, the dramatist and the actor, get their rights in this play, but the claims of the third part, the public, to a clearly intelligible, immediately comprehensible expression of the purposes of the author are not realized.

Ludwig called *Der Erbförster* a declaration of war against unnaturalness and the conventional fashion of present day poetry as well as of dramatic art. But there was lacking in the call to the people the convincing power to attract the great body to his standard, even if some of the best did applaud.

But one other work by Ludwig was put upon the stage in his lifetime, *Die Makkabäer* (1850–52). Again, after great wrestlings, the final form grew out of repeated remodellings of the rude material taken from the Bible. Originally, when the piece was still called *Die Makkabäerin*, the two hostile wives of Judah, the priest, were the central figures and his struggles formed only a background of extrinsic and opera-like liveliness. In the second revision the elder wife Leah was made the mother of Judah and opposed to her was his young wife Naomi, hated and despised. Greater importance is attached now to the contrast between Judah and his younger brother Eleazer, the vanity of whose mother wishes to place him on the throne of Jerusalem. From the broader foundation of this second version, by contraction and stronger emphasis on the dramatic, the last form of *Die Makkabäer* was constructed. As in the *Erbförster*, so also here conditions of time and place give the feeling that prevails throughout. Nowhere does the absolute, free Ego ap-

pear as with Schiller and his successors. The people
are closely bound up in the prejudices and peculiarities
of their race and age. This is shown especially and
conclusively in that the nation places itself blindly
under the dominion of the god which it created for
itself after its own image. From this belief comes the
strength of Judah and his family but also their destruction. The tragic fate of the great and simple hero
Judah arises from the fact that he cannot free his
people from the confining limits of this blind belief.

It is hard to see why Ludwig placed the mother
beside Judah as a martyr to the true faith, unless one
thinks of the history of the origin of the play. As it
now stands, one's sympathy vacillates undecided between the two chief characters and the action is forced,
picking its way with difficulty from the one to the other.
At the same time one also feels that in the dramatist's
mind the fate of the nation stands above their personal
fate as the more important. Here is another of those
beginnings of dramatic psychology of the masses such
as we find in Kleist's *Robert Guiskard* and Hebbel's
Judith. In his dissection and combination of the sum
total of instincts and feelings by means of single
speakers Ludwig is at least the equal of both. The
style of the *Makkabäer* allowed him to dispense with
the little devices of the *Erbförster*. The great tragic
effect would appear in its purity, were it not clouded
by the unevenness of the composition which arises from
the organic weakness of the drama. To this cause alone
is it to be ascribed that Ludwig's great work is so rarely
permitted to appear on the stage. Its subject, its
mature quiet beauty of form, its easily comprehended
fundamental motives of patriotism and of family in-

stinct, the simple heroism of Judah, the motherly devotion and passionate pride of Leah—all these are effective on the stage, easily comprehensible, and should arouse enthusiasm, although Ludwig avoided the cheap effects of the average dramatists of his time.

Excessive reflection, which caused him repeatedly to destroy what he had written, restrained Ludwig from publishing other dramatic works. The numerous seemingly finished plays and incomplete sketches found among his papers are a sad proof of how he wore out his powers in his struggle with this opposing element. If, for example, like Hebbel, he makes Agnes Bernauer the heroine of a tragedy, he first deduces her fate from an intrigue of her tricky lover so that she appears as a sort of Genoveva; then he hesitates whether the unequal marriage is to be unfortunate in itself or whether the power of the state and politics is to shatter the union; then again he decides to picture Agnes as blinded by vanity and ambition and only when the husband does not know what to think of her, does he let her purer love develop; finally he has this soul-union destroyed by higher state-interests, that is, he reached apparently the same solution as Hebbel. But while the latter, like the lion in the fable, only springs once upon the prey, whether he overpowers it or not, Ludwig circles round and round the desired object and keeps repeating his attack because he lacks confidence in his own strength and a simple accurate conception of his aim.

In vain have such competent editors as Ernst von Wildenbruch, Wilhelm Buchholz, Josef Lewinsky and Christian Otto attempted to save for the stage the seemingly completed drama, *Das Fräulein von Scudery*. The organic defect that, as in *Die Makkabäer*, the interest passes from the real hero to another character and also the epic nature of the short story by E. T. A. Hoffmann from which Ludwig got his material have destroyed the effect which the fine psychological motivation of the romantic incident deserved.

The question arises how Ludwig came to choose by preference just such subjects. The explanation lies in the fact that he was incited to replace by a greater variety of elementary motives that rich superficial life which through Schiller's influence had prevailed on the German stage, to its hurt it has been said, and which, because of the weakness of puny imitators and the influence of French models, had more and more supplanted character-drawing, deeper motivation and genuine dramatic life.

Just because Ludwig wished to make an improvement in this direction, he chose his subjects preferably from the same fields as his opponents; Wallenstein and Marino Falieri, Friedrich II and King Alfred of England, Mary Stuart and many similar historic and heroic figures, finally Tiberius Gracchus, all appeared to his vision but they did not take on any distinct form in spite of all the author's admonitions to himself, when he cried out, "Straight as a string, most simple and compact, concise, above all no ramifications to infinity, etc." In vain did he try to give life to those characters which had their origin in reflection, in vain did he continue to read Shakespeare so as not to fall into "the microscopical"; he could not rid himself of the "dotting and pointing" and at the same time he lost sight of the lines of direction. Ludwig really possessed but half of the special gifts which make the dramatist, but just that very portion which is for the most part less de-

veloped in German writers. He knew only too well
the technical conditions but when the sum total of these
conditions presented themselves to him in the moment
of creation, he lost the necessary directness and plastic
accuracy. Although he was a genuine and original
dramatist, he belonged after all to the representatives
of decadence who are not able to give art new thought
and new forms. Like Moses he saw his people wandering in the wilderness and tried by never-ending self-
observation to find the guide in his own breast, but the
signs failed repeatedly and he finally clung in despair
to the image of Shakespeare, which, as he believed, gave
him the firmest hold. Others also might certainly have
found support there but when his *Shakespeare-Studien*
appeared in 1871, no one seized the outstretched hand.

"THE SEVENTIES"

When German unity had been won back on the battle-
fields of France and the Empire been proclaimed again
at Versailles, people were hoping that for the stage
also, through a strong development of the national spirit,
a new period of prosperity would grow out of the same
enthusiasm which had revealed itself so overpoweringly
in battle. But the low condition of artistic education,
the preponderance of coarse materialism which celebrated its orgies in the years immediately following the
war and the complete exhaustion which, after the great
commercial crisis of 1873, lamed all effort, but above
all the demoralisation of the actor's art caused these
hopes to come to nought.

The plays of Goethe and Schiller were still given because of a sort of feeling of propriety, or to offer travel-

ling "stars" an opportunity to make use of their arts but there was in these performances a lack of any loving care, or any entering into the spirit of the writings while everything was ruthlessly cut out which did not give promise of an immediate outward effect.

At no time was there greater justice in the complaint of the more ambitious dramatists that the managers of the various theatres blocked their admittance. When here and there individual court-theatres opened their doors to works of the nobler class, this unusual favor was owing almost always to personal connection or to a hazy liking for the ideal on the part of the manager and therefore it mostly benefited only the amateurs.

Only very rarely did a greater talent arise and succeed in forcing his way through. ALBERT LINDNER won applause for his powerful Roman drama, *Brutus and Collatinus* (1866), and the Schiller-prize founded by King Wilhelm I of Prussia, but the expectations which this work aroused were not fulfilled afterwards and the author's life closed in insanity, a victim of vain effort.

ADOLPH WILBRANDT possessed a stronger nature and greater flexibility. He showed his fine artistic sense in pleasant comedies like *Die Maler* (1892), which were written in a form suitable for the stage. In the tragedies *Arria und Messalina* (1874) and *Nero* (1876) he portrayed, in the same style as his contemporary Makart, the real representative of the art of this period, scenes from luxurious Rome of Imperial days and in this way won the public that sought from the stage only sensuous charm.

Full of spirit but aiming too much at outward effects was the painter and poet, ARTHUR FITGER, in his *Hexe* (1876). Because of the boldness with which free thought, which was indeed not deep, was contrasted with dogma, the play caused a sensation and in certain circles was enthusiastically received. The colors are just as harsh as in Fitger's following works, *Von Gottes Gnaden* (1884) and *Die Rosen von Tyburn* (1888), which had no success on the stage.

With seeming psychological depth and outwardly modern expression RICHARD VOSS delineates by preference in his numerous dramas women of abnormal disposition: *Magda* (1875), *Mutter Gertrud* (1885), *Alexandra* (1886), *Eva* (1889). The clever construction and accurate calculation of effect could not, however, in the long run delude people into overlooking the painful character of his subjects and their innate unreality. In regard to his choice of subjects and his method of treatment Voss was strongly influenced by the French play of manners. The defeated of 1871 became the rulers on the German stage. Society of the Second French Empire had been reflected in that dramatic class whose chief representative was Alexander Dumas *fils*. Beginning with *La Dame aux Camélias* he had written a long succession of plays in which he delineated the upper circles of Paris with their moral unscrupulousness, their race after money and pleasure, their elegant men and women. With their halo of beauty and unmerited misfortune the fallen woman and the adulteress are glorified and as a problem of the highest importance for this society Dumas discusses from continually new standpoints the relation of *monde* and *demi-monde*. He generally puts his views in the mouth of an experienced man of the world who, with a superior air, looks down upon the doings of the rest and guides the action which is usually not very comprehensive but always exciting. The brilliant varnish of witty dialogue disguises the dramatic faults of the pictures which are mostly grouped about one large scene in which the opposing forces come together with a loud crash.

The skilful make-up of these plays, their frivolity, their *esprit* and their apparent freedom from narrow middle-class ethics exercised the greatest charm upon the audiences of German theatres. In Berlin and Vienna special theatres were built for them and in these there grew up a new and elegant style of dramatic art which, however, could not make up for the moral mischief produced by these glorifications of a degenerate and pleasure-loving society.

The operettas which crossed the Rhine were also filled with the same spirit. Their master, Offenbach, saturated the insinuating melodies with a bold contempt for everything noble and with the careless mirth of Parisian life. This class was also hailed with joy in Germany and fostered with great success in its own ''temples of art.'' French plays and French operettas won the lion's share of all triumphs in the seventies until Johann Strauss of Vienna created in his *Fledermaus* (1876) the Viennese operetta which, in the same spirit, contributed to the lightest kind of entertainment, but was better suited to German taste.

The efforts to do the same for the play resulted in failure, chiefly because luckily there was in Germany no society in the French sense, though in the larger cities some tendencies in that direction were growing up in the circles of the newly-rich.

PAUL LINDAU was most successful in sketching pictures from this society, with outlines in French style. In his first play, *Marion* (1869), the scene of which is laid in France, the defender of an honorable system of ethics is answered "Ethics! Ethics! Contact with the parvenues of the middle classes is poisoning our whole society." But in truth the types which he afterwards introduced on German soil in *Maria und Magdalena* (1872) and *Ein Erfolg* (1874) are after all for the most part only *parvenues*, who are supposed to represent a new plutocracy. The cleverness of the light conversation deluded people for a long time into overlooking the worthlessness of these plays and later also Lindau achieved in the same way many more momentary successes. So also could HUGO LUBLINER obtain recognition, at a time when art had sunk to its lowest depths, with his more harmless but also less clever plays, *Der Frauenadovkat* (1874), *Die Frau ohne Geist* (1879).

Hardly ever has there been in a highly civilized nation in an epoch of great national triumphs a stage that was so degenerate as the German of the seventies. As a proof the new works may be cited which appeared in the two best theatres of Berlin and Vienna in the year 1875. In the Royal theatre in Berlin these were:

Die Modelle des Sheridan, play in four acts by Lubliner.

Die Hermannsschlacht, by Kleist, revised for the stage by Genée.

Liebe für Liebe, play in four acts by Spielhagen.

Was ist eine Plauderei? "A bit of gossip" in one act by Gensichen.

Bogadil, comedy in one act by Murad Effendi.

Der Hauptmann von Kapernaum, farce in three scenes by Winterfeldt.

Der verlorene Sohn, comedy in one act by Ring.

Der Frauenadvokat, play in three acts by Lubliner.

Der Feind im Hause, tragedy in five acts by O. Roquette.

Komtesse Dornröschen, "family life" in one act by Duke Elimar von Oldenburg.

Marius in Minturnä, play in one act by Marbach.

Der Seelenretter, comedy in one act by Hedwig Dohm.

Der Zankapfel, farce in one act by Paul Lindau.

Die Frau für die Welt, play in five acts by Wichert.

Tante Therese, play in four acts by Paul Lindau.

Im Altertumscabinett, comedy in one act by O. Sigl.

Citronen, farce in four acts by Rosen.

In the same year the Imperial Burg-theatre in Vienna offered the following:

Die Versucherin, comedy in one act by G. von Moser.

Über die Mauer, comedy in one act by Najac.

Eine Geschichte aus Kentucky, comedy in two acts by W. Marr.

Liebe für Liebe, play in four acts by Spielhagen.

Parisina, tragedy by Mosenthal.

Das Trauerspiel des Kindes, play in two acts by Schlesinger.

Ein passionierter Raucher, farce in one act by Duke Elimar von Oldenburg.

Nero, tragedy in five acts by Adolf Wilbrandt.

Tante Therese, play in four acts by Lindau.

The number and still more the merit of these pieces is frightfully small and confirms unquestionably the statement made above.

In the year 1863 the "Schiller prize," intended for the best drama of the last three years, could still be given to an important work, Hebbel's *Nibelungen,* in 1866 it was assigned to Lindau's *Brutus and Collatinus,* a drama in which artistic purposes and power were at least recognisable. In 1869 it was given to Geibel's *Sophonisbe,* a play quite worthless from a dramatic standpoint, in 1872 and 1875 it could not be assigned at all and in 1878 Wilbrandt, Nissel and Anzengruber received it, not for definite plays but in acknowledgment of their pre-eminent talents.

LUDWIG ANZENGRUBER

In the list of authors of new plays for 1875 one looks in vain for the name of LUDWIG ANZENGRUBER, the third writer rewarded with the Schiller prize in 1878. Although he was the most gifted and the sanest dramatist of the seventies his plays were not given in the high-class theatres because, without the deceiving brilliance of traditional and beautiful form, they delineated life-like characters from the people and had their origin in the world of the suburban theatres of Vienna.

Anzengruber was descended from the peasantry of Upper Austria. Born in Vienna, Nov. 29, 1839, at five years of age he lost his father, himself a gifted writer, and grew up in poor circumstances under the care of his mother. He tried to make his way in the book-trade but the theatre attracted him with ever-increasing strength and for ten long years from the winter of 1859 he wandered through the Austrian provinces as an actor, experiencing on the trips all the misery connected with the calling of a strolling comedian. Then he found a modest post in the Vienna police-office and made up his mind to give up all ambition to become an artist and author, because all his efforts to find a shelter for the children of his muse had been without success.

But just at that time the religious agitation following the Vatican Council aroused anew in him the forcibly repressed desire to create and in 1870 he wrote *Der Pfarrer von Kirchfeld*. Afterwards he gave up his official position and lived in Vienna as author and journalist, unhappily married, severely tried by bodily suffering, without obtaining fitting recognition or the corresponding material rewards. When his friends were preparing to celebrate his fiftieth birthday and when the consciousness of his importance was beginning to dawn upon larger circles, he fell ill and was carried off by sudden death, Dec. 10, 1889.

In vain did Anzengruber attempt to accomplish anything in the traditional forms with plays in iambic measure or with middle-class drama in the High German. His talents and originality unfolded only in the environment of dialect, in the peasant- and folk-play. The peasant-play had long before become a popular offshoot of lower-class drama which, without any artistic purpose and with cheap expedients, aimed at outward success (cf. p. 54). With its mixture of rude jest and melodrama it served for light entertainment.

In Anzengruber as in lofty drama the great problems of humanity are discussed. The garments, in which before him only theatrically correct dummies had been seen, now clothe people of such genuine nature that in them great tragic conflicts can arise. He himself tells at the close of his capital peasant novel, *Der Sternsteinhof*, why he chose the peasant costume. "This is not the result of the simple belief that by this means peasants are to be won as readers, nor with the speculative purpose of paying court to a tendency that is coming more and more into vogue, but merely for the reason that the narrow sphere of action of country life has less effect upon the naturalness and originality of the characters; that the passions, expressed without reservation or but clumsily concealed, are more comprehensible, and that the evidence of how characters grow or deteriorate under the influence of destiny, or how they fight against it and decide their own and others' fate is easier to produce in a mechanism that lies open to the day, as it were, than in one enclosed in a double case, covered over with traceries and an ornamental dial: just as in the oldest, simplest and most effective stories heroes and princes were breeders of herds and land owners and their Treasurers and Chancellors swineherds.''

He understood most accurately the nature of the folk-play and would not allow himself to be deprived of the right to reform and instruct. ''For what does a person work, pray,'' he wrote to a friend, ''especially in the field of the folk-play, if he does not wish to instruct, to enlighten and to inspire? Let the tragedian and comedian of higher style follow after the beautiful alone, after the artistic ideal without any accessories. But the folk-play as far as I know, have read and seen, has at all times, according to the standard of prevailing opinion, combined the purpose of teaching with that of entertainment.''

This tendency is always dominated in Anzengruber's works by the loftier search for truth. He considers himself the priest of a religion which has only *one* Goddess, Truth, and only *one* myth, that of the Golden Age, not away back in the past, an object of vain dreams and longing,—no! reaching into and lighting up all the future, the single goal of all joyous anticipation and of all active effort.''

For Anzengruber truth is found where goodness is found. Men are bad if selfishness or prejudice blinds them or if mistaken reverence for old out-worn institutions hinders their aspirations after freedom, truth and purity. According to the degree of hurtfulness, the bad appears in the mirror of literature as harmless and comical or pernicious and tragic. In the most of Anzengruber's scenes both are intermingled, full of significance and mirth-provoking as in life, in Shakespeare and in Molière.

In his wanderings he had learned exactly the nature of theatrical effects. He satisfied the desire of the actors for effective rôles and knew how to employ accurately all the little stage-expedients. Of the dialect of the locality which is the scene of his plays he makes use only so far as it does not prevent the man of a different part of the country from understanding. With justice Berthold Auerbach praises the remarkable combination of natural and theatrical courage in Anzengruber.

Outwardly his plays are similar to the earlier Austrian peasant-comedies and Vienna folk-plays, but in reality he made his own forms. He knows only exemplars but no model, no school but merely teachers, no imitation but only a glad, free aspiration. The earlier authors always sketched the peasants and townspeople from one side only according as they required them for the needs of the conflicts which had their course in the narrow circle of ordinary feeling. Love, hate, magnanimity, avarice, shrewdness, narrowness, each for itself and without any personal coloring, are embodied and contrasted in definite figures and come into outward collision. Anzengruber, on the other hand, endowed his characters with a far richer and more complicated life, conditioned by the peculiar nature of each individual, which stood out prominently in a superabundance of special characteristics. He did not shut his peasants off from the world by a range of mountains. Everything that was stirring in the religious, social and political life of the present, made its way into the villages also and there excited storms similar to those at the centres of public life. But from behind the storm-clouds there shone out the sun of a firm belief in mankind, throwing its warm rays even into the souls of the unfortunate and despised.

Anzengruber banished pessimism. Almost every one of his dramas shows the way to happiness by the exercise of firm courage and clear judgment. The solution is affected as in the old style of folk-play, that is, the good are rewarded, the evil reformed; the outward course of the plot, however, is not the cause of the change, but that inherent fate which purifies men and leads them to self-knowledge.

With great effectiveness Anzengruber unites universal human qualities with class-attributes and the other fortuitous influences, so that the effect of each of the three factors is clearly distinguishable and all in common modify the course of destiny.

Because of all these excellencies, Anzengruber's best works have a claim to stand beside the writings of the greatest dramatists and yet he will certainly not be granted this place. As the son of a time which was hostile to the great, he sought to veil what was genuine and deep in his work with a touch of playfulness; he had to represent himself as less important than he really was and to endeavor to please a perverted public. It was Anzengruber's misfortune that he tried this repeatedly and yet after all retained so much of his original nature that he did not descend low enough for the spectators. Only after his death was his great aim recognised through the mask made necessary by his unhappy times.

Up to that time only his first work, *Der Pfarrer von Kirchfeld,* had become known, the great and lasting success of which was due more to accident than to the real merit of the play. It had its origin in the excitement which was stirred up in Catholic lands because of the promulgation of the doctrine of infallibility in 1870. With an all too clearly outspoken tendency, with a pathos of a superficial theatrical type, "Hell," the priest with the striking name, represents the cause of enlightenment. It was this character with its purposeful sermons to the public that had great influence when the play appeared and long afterwards.

In the episodes and in the figure of "Wurzelsepp" the later Anzengruber, who is master of every scenic detail, is already proclaimed. "Wurzelsepp" is the first of his thinking peasants. They are not philosophers who, with trained reasoning powers, look out over life from a high watch tower; their thinking has its origin in their feelings. Those of them who, because of illegitimate birth, are outcasts from the peasant's social order, or who are not willing to submit to the restraint of custom or dogma, experience in their own person the force of a power, the justice of which they do not understand. Out of this arises at first hatred and embitterment, but Anzengruber scatters in the deep furrows of the lacerated soul the seeds of a human love and there grows up a joy in being and a belief in the goodness of the world-spirit, revealing itself in nature.

In *Die Kreuzelschreiber* (1872), the cheerful companion-picture to *Der Pfarrer von Kirchfeld,* he has described this in most masterly fashion, in the person of Steinklopfer-Hans, the best of his village philosophers. He is armed against misfortune by the conviction of his intimate connection with the everlasting Ruler, who wisely guides all things for the benefit of the world. Therefore this world is for him, the poor and despised, a merry world. No harm can befall him, he belongs to the universal and the universal to him. In this glad certainty he finds his solution, when the peasants, carried away by the trend of the times, thoughtlessly rebelled against the church, and the women, urged on by the priest, thereupon renounce their marital duties until the offense is atoned for by a pilgrimage to Rome. In these really comical conflicts appeared, peculiarly distorted, the great universal contrasts: the power of tradition against which genuine aspiration for freedom and indiscreet desire for innovation alike fight in vain. The farcical merry comedy is a not unworthy companion-piece to the *Lysistratus* of Aristophanes. The fate of old Brenninger, harried to death by the breakdown of lifelong customs, admonishes one of the deep seriousness underlying the bright play.

While Anzengruber also attempted in *Der Pfarrer von Kirchfeld* to give the peasant play greater value by an outspoken didactic tendency, he now took the right way to raise the class into the domain of genuine art by giving greater depth to the conflicts, by describing the circumstances which decide them and by a more detailed characterization. At the same time his courage for truth had grown very considerably. His first play, for the sake of theatrical conventionalities, had still carefully avoided everything objectionable and shunned the little traits serving merely to give an impression of complete fidelity to life, because the prevailing theory of art banished from the drama all naturalistic description as well as everything accidental and unimportant for the outward course of the action. Now he fairly revelled in the accurate observation of these details and the great brawl at the close of the third act gave evidence for the first time on the German stage of the power of an art opposed to the old ideals of beauty.

Anzengruber had prepared the transition to this new art in his second work, *Der Meineidbauer* (1871). Like Shakespeare's Richard III, Matthias Ferner, the cross-roads-farmer, had risen by crime and maintained his high position with unfeeling harshness by means of new crimes. He is in his way just as great a man as the royal murderer of Britain and, like him, with brazen front opposes avenging fate, which naturally employs in this play meaner and more objectionable devices than in the great tragedy.

In the speech and manners of the characters of the *Meineidbauer* there is still a good deal that is conventional, but the technique is remarkably new, lifting gradually one veil after another from the past, so that along with men and things from the present their evolution with its conditioning causes becomes clear. The impression of compulsory necessity which is thus called forth permits one to see more easily the sway of chance in the last stages of the action which are transferred to the stage.

Anzengruber again gave the serious picture of the *Meineidbauer* a cheery companion when in 1874 he composed *Der G'wissenswurm*. Here there is also a criminal who, however, allows himself to be tormented by qualms of conscience instead of stifling them, like *Der Meineidbauer,* until it is shown that his worries are only imaginary and artificially nourished by a selfish, legacy-hunting hypocrite. The meeting with his former loved one, whom he had thought wretched and ruined, and whom he now finds again, abounding in strength and contented as the mother of twelve children, is a capital invention of the poet; so also the true-hearted girl who, in spite of the fact that she knows neither father nor mother, has such a joyous outlook on life.

The purest embodiment of the joy of life among Anzengruber's work is the peasant-farce, *Doppelselbstmord* (1875), a worthy dramatic companion-piece to Keller's short story *Romeo und Julia auf dem Dorfe.* The son of the rich man loves the daughter of the poor man and they go to the "*Alm* to be united forever." The double sense of these words leads the father of the lad and the other villagers astray and all night they hunt anxiously for the fugitives. With their mistake vanish also all hostile feelings.

Love in the abstract, shy and awkward of expression, is revealed in the youthful couple. It is true poetry without all the beautiful words and metaphors esteemed necessary by earlier writers. Their place is taken by inherent beauty, which bursts forth out of a rough shell, and most touchingly where life itself has made it hard, as is the case with the old carriage-jobber, the father of the girl, who with his words *"'s is a Dummheit"* (it's all nonsense) pretends to take no real interest in things, while at the same time his heart is full of love and sympathy. Never did Anzengruber combine so intimately as in this play the mixture of love of life and life's seriousness, the tragic contrasts of the true world and its diverting superficial manners. Yet success was denied him. Prudery, according to August Wilhelm Schlegel "the pretention to innocence without innocence," took offence at the naïvetê of the farce. Anzengruber himself was partly to blame for that, because he yielded so far to the demands of the ordinary public that it might be thought the poet himself had wished to pander to depraved tastes in the choice of his subject.

The very same is true of his next farces which are furnished with a little less juicy heart, *Der ledige Hof* (1876), which sacrifices a tragic and grand woman character to the purpose of providing merriment at all costs, *'s Jungferngift* (1878), and *Die Trutzige* (1878).

Through lack of success the poet became uncertain. Even before this he had tried to leave his own field for that of higher-class drama, e. g., in *Elfriede* (1872), *Bertha von Frankreich* (1872-74), *Die Tochter des Wucherers* (1873) and *Ein Faustschlag* (1877). In them he aimed at presenting characters from the people in the midst of the bustle of the large city, by which they are estranged from nature. The cheery, unassuming lower classes of old Vienna, whose portrait Raimund had once placed before their very eyes, were dying out. A new race was growing up, without the feeling of class-honor, without energy of endeavor, anxiously pursuing mere enjoyment. Modest competency, respectability and the religious sense vanished when the ethical foundation was gone from beneath their feet. The commandment, "Honor thy father and thy mother," loses its validity when the parents are not worthy of reverence. Anzengruber's *Viertes Gebot* (1877) shows this by one example each from the lower and upper classes, from the family of the lazy turner Schalanter and of the rich landlord Hutterer. In both the daughters are sold, the sons spoiled by their education and only where good old customs watch faithfully over the children does parental love become a blessing to them. Not only morally but physically the new generation is being ruined by the sins of the old. Anzengruber represents all this in a plot which occupies a remarkable middle-place between the old folk-play with its rich external happenings but poor argumentation, and the new psychological drama which is poor in plot. Scenes of strong and affecting fidelity to nature alternate with others full of sentimental bliss and false pathos. Instead of one simple straight plot we see three running along side by side, crossing one another only at certain points as chance may offer. A style in which to represent the inherent necessity of the incidents had not yet been found but the beginnings of it are mighty enough to cause an unusually potent influence to proceed from the work. Its independence in the face of the prevailing hypocritical morality, its attack upon the absolute nature of one of the Ten Commandments, and its detailed description of the depraved were, however, for *Das vierte Gebot* greater hindrances on the stage than its own organic weakness. And yet it is easy to see that the poet did not allow the lower instincts to rule absolutely because of joy in what was ugly. His characters are not blindly given over to one destiny, their fate is not conditioned by natural law, education or society. A firm will and a joyous faith in goodness can lift them out of vice and misery. This conviction is clearly set forth in the three less important Vienna plays by Anzengruber, *Die alten Wiener* (1878), *Brave Leut' vom Grund* (1879), and *Heimgefunden* (1885).

Anzengruber then returned once more to his old field in his last drama, *Der Fleck auf der Ehr'* (1877). An innocent peasant girl has come under suspicion of theft and is ruined because the sense of honor of her class count the suspicion which brought her to prison as an inexpiable sin. As with the "children of sin" of his earlier works, so here we find a fate which destroys happiness where no guilt is present and only outwardly is a happy ending brought about by an improbable accident. The poet's accuracy in the use of technical devices can not delude one into overlooking the poverty of material and the inconsistency of the solution.

The last plays by Anzengruber prove that through constant battling with the decadent dramatic art of his day, he had become discouraged and had lost his naïve freedom in creative work. It is idle to ask whether he would have found it again, if a share had been granted him in the fresh goodwill which in the very year of his death was directed to that serious drama which was aiming to get away from tradition and make an advance.

THE MEININGER

In the year 1880 Anzengruber cried plaintively, "We have no longer a stage," and certainly he had a right to this crushing judgment when he glanced at the doings of the regular German theatres. Their activity was governed by hollow idealism and ordinary business-sense. But in two different directions the desire to make improvements had already been made manifest in deeds and with convincing success: on the circuits of the Meininger and in Richard Wagner's Bayreuth festival-plays.

In May, 1874, the court players of the Duke of Meiningen began their first "starring" in Berlin with the performance of *Julius Cæsar*. The surprising impression made by this drama, long known and naturalized on the stage, was due to the carrying through of this one principle; everything to be subordinated to the purposes of the poet and these to be realized by summoning all the devices of dramatic art and of modern stage-technique. The result of this was first, outwardly the most conscientious observance of historical setting in scenery and costumes. With such care and such great expense as had up to that time been expended on the opera alone, the Meininger provided for each individual drama a suitable artistic setting and by this means gave a new sensuous charm to the classic plays. The fear that, because of extrinsic brilliancy, attention would be diverted from the work itself, was very soon proven false, because it was shown that dramas of ideal type were brought nearer to the interest and understanding of the present by this very realistic and faithful historic background.

The second important innovation of the Meininger was that of driving out the "Star" system. All actors, from the highest to the lowest, had to place themselves unreservedly at the service of the whole artistic production, which by oneness of purpose grew out of drama, performance and scenery. No one might refuse to take over the smallest rôle. The performance of each individual actor was brought to the greatest perfection in numberless rehearsals by the conductor of the play, the Duke of Meiningen himself, and then with those of the other actors and of the carefully trained troops of supernumeraries blended together to a complete unit with just as indefatigable labor.

This hitherto unknown conscientiousness was above all of great advantage to Schiller's dramas, the playing of which had been quite neglected. They gained a new and unexpected influence. The passionate energy of the great mass-scenes of *Die Räuber,* of *Fiesco,* of *Wallenstein* and of *Die Jungfrau von Orleans* had never up to that time been felt so strongly, the structure of the dramatic framework never so clearly seen and admired in its artistic completeness. No longer the brilliant showpieces, the great monologues, but the hitherto unnoticed ensemble-scenes which develop the real dramatic elements appeared as the climaxes.

For seventeen years, from 1874–1890, the Meininger travelled through Germany and a number of other countries, giving in this period 41 plays and 2,591 performances. They displayed their new art most successfully in Schiller's and Shakespeare's dramas, but did not shun the modern writers, as their experiments with various works by Ibsen, Björnson, Lindner, Fitger and Echegaray give proof.

When they gave up their trips their mission was fulfilled. The new dramatic art had become the common property of all theatres making any claim to artistic rank. True, only rarely indeed was there to be found the same lofty seriousness, the same expenditure of time and means and the same capacity for personal self-sacrifice as with them; besides, the conditions of the regular theatres scarcely ever allowed of such intense attention to one work. At the same time the right relation of the individual factors of dramatic art were once more restored. The author was again given the chief place, the conductor took his place beside him as his representative and interpreter, and the selfishness, vanity and laziness of the actors, as well as the business-sense of the directors, had to be subordinate to both. So far as means at all permitted, the public and critics now demanded a faithful observance of historic truth, a conscientious study of each individual rôle and well rounded ensemble-play.

Not only was new life breathed into the masterpieces of old style by these principles, but the stage could now offer to writers trying other roads actors who were more tractable and better trained for their duties.

RICHARD WAGNER

The fundamental thought that all arts must work together in the service of the writer in order to obtain the greatest effect for a drama had been uttered by RICHARD WAGNER long before the appearance of the Meininger and was overwhelmingly and grandly exemplified when under his guidance his *Ring des Nibelungen* was first performed in 1876 at Bayreuth.

In 1813, E. T. A. Hoffmann wrote an essay entitled *Der Dichter und der Komponist* in which he expressed the conviction that Romantic opera is the only true opera, because the music must necessarily have its origin directly in the poetry, and that, because of these conditions, musical drama must originate as the work of a gifted and really romantic poet. "I maintain," he says in this essay, "that the opera writer, just as well as the musician, must compose everything as it were in his soul and it is only the clear consciousness of certain melodies, indeed of certain tones of the accompanying instruments, in a word, the easy command of the spiritual field of tones which distinguishes the latter from the former."

In the same year in which these words were written, as if meant for him, Richard Wagner was born at Leipzig, May 22, 1813. In Dresden he conceived an admiration for Weber, then at Leipzig felt the influence of the French and Italian music fashionable there. Its sentiment, happy even to frenzy and to sensual frivolity, appealed to his strong physical nature and in the style of Auber and Bellini, after some imitative attempts, he wrote in 1834 his opera, *Das Liebesverbot oder die Novize von Palermo,* after Shakespeare's *Measure for Measure.* In the very same style as "Young Germany," he glorifies the victory of free sensuousness over puritanical hypocrisy. Wagner was at that time friendly with Heinrich Laube and in his *Zeitung für die elegante Welt* he expressed for the first time his requirements from the German opera.

Then followed years of travel, full of wretchedness until he found a permanent position as bandmaster at Riga (1837–39). For his great artistic views and his

liberal political ideas he sought artistic expression in
the opera, *Reinzi, der letzte der Tribunen,* the material
for which he took from Bulwer-Lytton's novel. The
false brilliancy of Meyerbeer's art had dazzled him,
too, in those days so that he tried to imitate its outward
form. But the accuracy and conciseness of the dramatic
construction, the genuine passion and the poetic thought
of the opera distinguishes his work from the cool, calculating ''grand opera'' of the French and Italians.

In vain did Wagner hope, when he went to Paris in
1840, to get his *Rienzi* performed by Meyerbeer's aid
and he suffered great distress. At this time he turned
away from this false art which he now attacked in
numerous essays after the style of E. T. A. Hoffmann.
He became again a German Romanticist and *Der
fliegende Holländer,* which took form in 1841 at Meudon,
followed Weber and Marschner directly, especially *Der
Vampyr* and *Hans Heiling.* He saturated the simple
thrilling legend, acquaintance with which he owes to
Heinriche Heine, with the opposing principles of sensual
love and of sympathy which impels to an expiatory
death in behalf of the lover. Like the ballads of the
northern people, the opera is a string of single, quickly
passing, garishly illumined pictures, which gleam up
like ghosts before the dark background of a mysterious
fate.

In 1842 Wagner returned to Germany and *Tannhäuser* took form in Dresden in 1843–45. Tieck had
already connected the story of the old Tannhäuser poem
with the legend of *Der getreue Eckart,* Hoffmann with
that of the *Sängerkrieg* on the Wartburg. Heinrich
Heine, in his parody of the old poem, had endowed

Tannhäuser with the longing which drives him out of the joys of the Venus-mountain back to earth.

Influenced by Hoffmann and Heine, Richard Wagner, by an effective change of the closing part, added the moral, religious and redeeming power of a pure virgin's love and gave it form in the fictitious character of the prince's daughter, to whom he gave the name of St. Elizabeth. Thus out of the old opera which appealed only to the senses there was made a problem-drama which enlists music in the service of spiritual development.

This happened in a still greater degree in *Lohengrin*, composed immediately afterwards. Here, too, the old legend is filled with a new content: Elsa's love asks from the unknown, for whom she feels admiration and gratitude, that she may know him fully in order to devote herself entirely to him; but the god dare not reveal himself to the mortal woman, else she would die under his glance. As Semele is destroyed by her wish to see Jupiter in his divine majesty, so Elsa is destroyed by the loftiest of desires, having its foundation in the essence of love.

Weber's *Euryanthe* had given the models for the characterization of the gloomy figures Ortrud and Telramund, the great court-scene in Marschner's *Der Templer und die Jüdin* had a great influence on the first act, the quarrel between the queens in the Nibelungen-epic gave the principal motive and many details for the great scene of the bridal procession. And yet as a whole the opera was the spiritual property of Wagner and gave evidence of his independence in all essential points, his lofty view of the work of a dramatist and the ability, shown by no one before him, to combine the devices of music and of poetry in the service of this work.

The complete break with the old rigid forms of music was now accomplished. The declamation was not hindered by the melody but rather increased in effectiveness to the loftiest possibility of dramatic expression, the combinations of moods and the succession of thoughts were disclosed in the orchestra, what is unexpressed and inexpressible stood revealed. There resulted a new management and interweaving of melodies, the understanding of which was difficult for the untrained ear and the sensuous beauty of which was not apparent at the first hearing.

For this reason Wagner's new style was at first rejected with ridicule and anger by the great majority of musicians and laymen and it was a bold act when his faithful friend Franz Liszt produced *Lohengrin* for the first time in Weimar, Aug. 28, 1850. From the place which had witnessed the rebirth of higher-class drama began the victorious march of German opera. Schiller's hopes were fulfilled, that out of the opera, as out of the choruses of the old Bacchus-festival, tragedy would develop in a nobler form.

Wagner was not concerned merely about the purification of the musical part. Like Hebbel he desired to make the drama the image of the inner world of the poet and the receptacle of the loftiest and deepest impulses of the present, to combine philosophical, political and social purposes. Music was to him only a means to help give expression to the unconscious and to increase the power of the senses to give impressions. Therefore he could, as he went on, think of dispensing with this aid and plan spoken dramas, like *Friedrich der Rotbart, Jesus von Nazareth, Wieland der Schmied* and *Achilleus,* which were not indeed completed because mighty influences soon directed him once more to the opera.

Wagner took part in the Revolution of 1849 in the belief that through it his artistic purposes would be furthered. He had to flee and the following years of banishment were given to the philosophical foundation and superstructure of his views on art. He had found his guide in the philosopher Ludwig Feuerbach. According to him religion originated in the desire for happiness; the gods were the reflected images of men, the ideals of the people who gave them form. This theory had a mighty influence upon Wagner, just as it had on Gottfried Keller, for it recognized joyously and consciously the truth of sense-perception and extolled death as the last and greatest right of the living, the real conclusion of existence. Hostile to Christian dogma, he took refuge in the antique world of beauty which Anselm Feuerbach, Ludwig's brother, had described in his book, *Der Vatikanische Apollo.*

He did not, however, look at this depraved world with fruitless complaints about a lost ideal but with a strong desire to cause a new humanity to arise which should be worthy of it. In antique tragedy he saw the reflex of a free people fully developed in all directions. Here all the arts, plastic, mimic and rhetorical, work together to the highest aims. Through Christianity, as Wagner at that time supposed, mankind had fallen into slavery; Art, in the service of the church, of princes and of industry, had degenerated to handicraft and now served only the few as a sensual enjoyment and luxury. Only when at some future time the great revolution of mankind has uprooted slavery in every form, can the rebirth of the drama take place. In this *Kunstwerk der Zukunft*, the sole subject of which is a beautiful and strong humanity, which has attained to freedom by the loftiest power of love, all the individual arts are most intimately connected as in classic tragedy. It appeals to the whole people out of whose life in common it had its issue as the loftiest intellectual production. Wagner developed these thoughts in a number of works written in Zurich, viz: *Kunst und Klima* (1850), *Das Kunstwerk der Zukunft* (1850), *Oper und Drama* (1851).

Even before this he had written the drama which, on a national basis, embodied this idea and also the means for its realization. In the year 1848 *Siegfrieds Tod* was written, in 1851 its sunny companion-picture, *Der junge Siegfried,* appeared, and in the following year Wagner wrote, first *Walküre* and then *Rheingold*, because of the necessity of developing independently the mythical and philosophical foundations of the action. After *Siegfrieds Tod* had been remodelled into *Götterdämmerung,* to fit in with the three other plays in preparation, Wagner had the principal work printed for his friends towards the end of 1852. He called it *Der Ring des Nibelungen, ein Bühnenfestspiel für drei Tage und einen Vorabend*. The music of *Rheingold* was already finished in 1854, *Walküre* in the beginning of 1856, but in the middle of *Siegfried,* in 1857, work ceased and only after a long pause was it completed in 1869, and *Die Götterdämmerung* in 1874. In his work, *Die Nibelungen,* which appeared in the same decade, Hebbel had used almost exclusively the German folk-epic as his source, but Wagner gave the northern version of the Edda commanding consideration. Out of it he tried to extract the essence of the old legend and conceived of it as mythical and not historical. He considered Siegfried synonymous with the Germanic god Baldur whose death symbolizes the destruction of the world. It must be destroyed because the greed for possession and power has become dominant and has also ensnared and poisoned the representatives of purity, *Wotan* and the *Lichtalben*. Their ending is prepared for them by the dark Nibelungs and in vain does Wotan beget for himself Siegmund, the hero who shall conquer the enemy. Siegfried alone, not begotten by the guilt-laden god, but a free innocent man, is able to snatch away the ring, the symbol of power and possession, from the guardian dragon. But he also becomes involved in guilt through Hagen, the son of Nibelung, and with him is destroyed Brunhild, the daughter of the god, who in her selfishness wishes to live only for her love. Walhall, the citadel of the gods, flashes up in flames and the ring is given back to the daughters of the Rhine, from whom Nibelung had once stolen his gold. The great wealth of thought and the dramatic significance of the ring lift the drama into the domain of genuine and lofty tragedy, but the whimsical outer form of the senselessly applied alliteration, the purposely archaic language, distorted by countless puns and the tendency to extended expositions, which do not advance the dramatic action, detract from the artistic merit. The characterization also is often weakened by the symbolic conception of the figures.

At the close of the *Ring* the sin-laden world goes down to destruction and finds peace in ruin. This corresponds to the new views which Wagner had come to independently and had found confirmed in the philosophy of Schopenhauer. His lack of success in his efforts and the necessity of giving up his relation to the high-minded Mathilde Wesendonk had driven him to pessimism, all hope in the future had vanished and the thought of contempt for and victory over the world was a deliverance for him. Everything in his earlier works he now declared to be the product of a very abnormal condition and from the view-point of this new world philosophy he composed *Tristan und Isolde* (1854), the "song of songs" of a love perfected in death.

Once more the legend became the receptacle of his personal view-point. In the epic of Tristan and Isolde Gottfried von Strassburg had extolled the good fortune of a "love of high degree" and surrounded it with the richest fullness of life. Wagner extracted from it the fundamental tragic motives, the unconquerable desire for the woman whom Tristan has wooed for his lord and father's friend, with the determination to give up his own claim to her. The magic love-potion does not awaken their love. On the contrary, both had felt from the very beginning that they were destined for one another; they do not intend treason but a mortal longing is the torment which they suffer. The number of external incidents is here limited to those absolutely necessary, so that the fundamental lyric feelings may have complete course. The poet revels in them and spreads over them all the charms of lofty poetry into which the contemplative is this time completely merged.

Not for long could Wagner's active and really joyous, sensuous nature remain in this state of pessimism. When in the summer of 1860 he returned to Germany and could look with more confidence into the future, he worked out an old plan of his Dresden days and wrote in 1862 his *Meistersinger von Nürnberg.*

The peaceful German Imperial city, filled with genuine cheeriness, in which Hans Sachs had written, became the scene of a capital comedy. The antagonism between a limited philistine art and gifted creative work is embodied most happily in the school-laws of the tablature, restored true to history, and in the independent song of Walther von Stolzing. Without obtrusiveness the poet also gave free course to his disgust with his opponents. Unaffected by these purposes, the characters unfold and are full of life, while the course of the happily invented love-intrigue is intimately connected with the clash of view-points in art.

When Wagner had finished the musical composition for this work in 1867, there was already looming up, through a surprising intervention of destiny, an early prospect of the fulfilment of his boldest plans which up to that time had seemed unattainable. The young king of Bavaria, Ludwig II, showed him his favor and, with the aid of a rapidly increasing host of enthusiastic supporters, he was able to build his festival-theatre in Bayreuth, where, far from "the daily round," the drama, by a new art of presentation and under a pure and ideal fostering care, was to awaken an exaltation and enthusiasm worthy of its high calling.

In the presence of the German emperor and of a number of princes, the *Ring des Nibelungen* was given here for the first time in August, 1876, and in defiance to the slack and degenerate spirit of the times won a success, which, exerting a continuous influence even beyond German boundaries, has given an impulse to the purification of the artistic spirit and to a revolt from the frivolity of the old opera.

In continual conflict with the "business" sense, with indolence and the encouragement of search after low pleasure, the mightiest factors in the life of the regular theatres, Bayreuth, even since the death of Wagner, holds high the banner of the practice of pure art, and for it fortunately the last and profoundest work of the master, *Der Parsifal* (1882), has up to the present been reserved.

In Parsifal pessimism has become clarified to sympathy and there appears a new ideal for the future, an ethical regeneration of the world by a recognition of its woes. The most thoughtful poem of the German Middle Ages, Wolfram von Eschenbach's *Parcival,* is here, as was Gottfried von Strassburg's *Tristan* in the former opera, carried back to its simplest elements and over it a mystical splendor is shed, so that the vicarious suffering of Christ in the person of the hero, along with his own suffering, becomes the salvation of mankind. Amfortas, the King of the Grail, who is freed from his torments by Parsifal, had been wounded with the same lance which once pierced the Redeemer's side and Herodias lives on in Kundry, the messenger of the Grail.

The sin of the hero is ignorance of suffering, which refuses sympathy; through sympathy he attains to understanding without guilt. Because of this there is lacking in the drama everything that otherwise forms a basis in tragic conflicts and in its temper it consciously approaches the oratorio, the character of which also prevails in the music. Even if this coloring were demanded by the peculiar nature of the material, it yet gives evidence of declining powers and does not permit the last lofty work of Wagner to appear as the equal of the earlier dramas. Perhaps this was contributed to by the suffering which overtook him even while he was working at *Parsifal,* and to which he succumbed, Feb. 13, 1883.

With Wagner's last works is closed for the present the history of the musical drama of Germany. Neither in the old forms nor in the new ones created by him has there a work appeared which can offer anything fresh in respect to drama and the present day is still living entirely on its inheritance from the great age of opera which began with Gluck and has ended, as it seems, with Wagner.

ERNST VON WILDENBRUCH

The salutary influence of the *Meininger* on the stage and the public, the interest in the enjoyment of a noble art, which has been awakened by them and Richard Wagner, was first of advantage to ERNST VON WILDENBRUCH, a poet who for ten long years had been knocking in vain at the portals of the theatre with his dramas of an ideal tendency. In May, 1881, the *Meininger* brought his tragedy, *Die Karolinger,* upon the boards at their home, in the autumn of the same year a Berlin theatre repeated the attempt amid the greatest applause and then his earlier rejected tragedies appeared in rapid succession in all the larger theatres. In him seemed to have been found the long wished for successor of Schiller, who was to bring release from the wretched drama of the last decades.

Carried away by the strong passionate flight of his poetry, the public overlooked the weaknesses in the confused plot, the insufficient motivation and the superficial psychology. The poet did not allow his hearers to recover consciousness so long as he held them in his spell and it was seen that the seemingly worn-out forms of the old historical drama again and again prove their power, whenever a strong individuality and an ideal temperament give them the corresponding contents and whenever the desire for brilliant pictures, for strong momentary effects is fulfilled.

On looking closer, however, one recognizes that Wildenbruch's enthusiastic temperament was not kindled by warm spiritual conflict. Settled in his moral and patriotic convictions, he scarcely feels the deep discord running through his times, however much trouble he gives himself to comprehend and represent the movements of the present. Over his first dramas lay the rosy glimmer of a simple youthful belief in ideals which had not yet been dimmed by experience. The hope has not been fulfilled that he would struggle upwards out of this beginner's stage which is best embodied in *Die Karolinger* (1882), *Harold* (1882), *Der Mennonit* (1884) and *Das neue Gebot* (1886).

Even *Die Haubenlerche* (1891), which tries to make connection with the realistic drama of the present, aims at proving his good faith in the well-regulated mechanism of the course of the world with its righteous division of reward and punishment, only that the pathos disguises itself in Berlin dialect and the people do not wear historical dress. Wildenbruch gained his greatest and most lasting triumph with this play because he succeeded in infusing into the scenes from lowly life a lofty, inspiring and yet human spirit which the majority of dramatists misused for mere formal experiments. But his own particular field is the historical drama which places external scenes before the eyes of the spectator with superficial argumentation and above all tries to cause strong excitement through interest in the subject.

Subjects from the history of Brandenburg and Prussia lay nearest to hand for this enthusiastic patriot and, as Raupach had once done for the Hohenstaufens, so now Wildenbruch has put the Hohenzollerns on the stage in a series of historical pictures and of faithful portraits. But in this he is not guided, like his predecessors, by the purpose of using the stage to supplement the teachings of history, but in his veins there courses a glowing love, admiration, and gratitude to the sovereigns who have by their sturdy deeds made little Brandenburg the cradle of the modern German Empire.

About the heads of these rulers there gathers all glory in the Hohenzollern dramas, *Die Quitzows* (1888), *Der Generalfeldoberst* (1889), and *Der neue Herr* (1891). The dramatic life of the characters is a failure because of the conviction that all opposition to the mission of the Hohenzollern is unjustifiable in itself and must be unsuccessful.

Wildenbruch does not, however, deserve the reproach of servility. His noble enthusiasm is far removed from the commanded glorification in the showy festival plays of Joseph Lauff, who otherwise proves himself to be a sane, sympathetic nature, as in his comedy, *Der Heerohme* (1902), or the voluntary place-hunting of importunate "patriotic" poets. Wildenbruch gained later a great but temporary success with the double drama,

Heinrich und Heinrichs Geschlecht (1896). The historical contrast of Germany's monarchial principles and the Papacy on the one hand and the conflict of the king against the egoism and separatism of German princes on the other, are the motive forces of those histories. The poet did not succeed, however, in translating the political motives into human ones nor in avoiding the impression of chance in the course of the historical events. In addition to this, he has in this drama still oftener than before brought in theatrical effects and is not able to hold fast the lines of characterization even in the rudest outlines. The weakening of his power in the later acts, which is a special characteristic of Wildenbruch, is seen very clearly in his latest drama, *König Laurin* (1902). The beginning of the action in the first act is significant and exciting but it flattens out quickly into a play of intrigue and proceeds fitfully and capriciously from one startling scene to another.

Actuated by the noblest purposes, endowed with the valuable qualities of a strong temperament and of an accurate eye for what is suited to the stage, Wildenbruch's talent has after all brought little good to German drama. Each of his successes means only a personal victory to the detriment of those efforts which are aimed at developing the psychical and strengthening the contact with the life of the present.

GERMAN DRAMA FROM 1885–1900

THE OLD ART AND NATURALISM

BASED on the conviction that classic antiquity has left behind it in all realms of art works that will forever remain standard, the view has been prevalent since the Renaissance that perfection is only to be attained by following these models. The history of modern German poetry up to the present is the history of its relation to antiquity. Its different periods are distinguished in this, that sometimes the outward form, sometimes the whole intellectual world of antiquity is to be acquired. Sometimes the effort is made to deny the present and become wrapped up in the antique, sometimes to combine the views of antiquity with modern ideas.

Classic art represents the last stage of this road and all the attacks of the Romanticists, of "Young Germany" and of the partisans of Realism down into the eighties were scarcely able to give the dominion of the art-view established by the classicists a passing shock, let alone to overthrow it.

The reason for this was partly that the great German writers had with the greatest ability perfected this style in their masterpieces and that the form was then given credit for the elevating effect which for the most part depended upon quite personal characteristics of Goethe and Schiller. But even in themselves Schiller's idealism and the plastic ideal of form in the mature Goethe possess a high ethical and artistic value. Both correspond entirely to the chief tendencies of the intellectual development of Germany since the Reformation. They represent the elevation of the body of German citizens from a modest existence through a striving for individual development and the highest ethical maturity to a freedom gained by will power because they are filled with faith in the realm of ideals and in the absolute nature of ethical demands.

The low, the ugly and the immoral find no place in this art where, as a justifiable power, they might have held their own, and passion had to allow itself to be shut in by the barriers of the prevailing ethical system or be dashed to pieces against them. The finer subjective characteristics of the psychical yield precedence entirely to typical qualities and are considered whimsical and abnormal. To the heroes was given a purified sentiment and a high culture which, indifferent to historical facts, permeated all with the same idealism and expressed itself always in the same noble, exalted language, with scarcely any shade of personal coloring. It was the business of the drama in the first place to impress upon the spectators the great teachings of history by sensuous representation, where some important incident was shown in its causes and development and in which those concerned pronounced ethical judgment upon themselves. Only the past, however, permitted such a seemingly final judgment, and the nearer one came to the present, the less could one fail to recognize that reality did not allow of such clear knowledge. For this reason classic art excluded the present from the field of serious drama and allowed it merely to present entertaining scenes without any higher purpose. Even here, however, the laws of that theory of beauty were held to be valid which admitted only what was pleasing to the eye and the feelings.

It is clear that this art is especially adapted to awakening enthusiasm for everything noble and grand, to strengthening in the people the belief in the ideal and to providing pure and lofty enjoyment.   In it are reflected the best qualities of German character and its imperishable significance depends upon the fact that it repeatedly embodies in noble form the victory of the free moral will over necessity.

And yet it cannot be denied that to fulfil its office, it simplified the universe altogether too much, did not venture to tread the mysterious regions of the inner life and paid too exclusive attention to the conscious impulses taking form in powerful action.

Idealism, upon which it depended, was crowded out in the course of the nineteenth century by other philosophical conceptions of first principles, especially by Pessimism and Materialism. The natural sciences gained a decisive influence upon thought because of which the universe was put out of joint. The spirit no longer appeared to be the independent sovereign of matter but bound to it indissolubly and conditioned by it in its being. Recognition of the historical, geographical and social relativity of all phenomena limited extraordinarily the assumption of personal freedom and in the place of the earlier simple hypotheses came now the co-operation of highly complicated factors, to which was assigned an absolute power, in accordance with natural laws.

Because of this, historical events also appeared in a different light, no longer as a series of great heroic deeds, but as a necessary result of industrial and psychical mass-movements in which the highest as well as the lowest must take part because everywhere the same inviolable laws hold sway.

The earlier standards of the essential and the non-essential, derived from the ethical estimate of personality, were rejected and in vain did historic science and philosophy look for new and universally accepted values.

As a result of this confusion, the new art sought at first to reproduce only external phenomena as conscientiously as possible and, in order to avoid the suspicion of an independent valuation in the old sense, preferred now those very subjects which, according to the earlier estimate, were considered distasteful to art and without significance, and to which, in addition, there clung the charm of novelty.

With the intensified curiosity of an explorer who penetrates into an untrodden district of Africa the material and psychical life of the proletariat, the prostitutes and the criminals was observed and described, without subjective coloring, as far as possible like an object in natural science.

This procedure was called Naturalism. Long before there was talk of this tendency in Germany it had become dominant in France and from there had exercised an influence, especially in Scandinavia and Russia. Even Romanticism in France, in contrast with that of Germany, had become extremely progressive and democratic in political matters. It inclined to the social conception which had given rise to a new art of story-telling in Balzac's novels. Upon the foundation laid by him built the great masters Gustav Flaubert and

Emil Zola. The latter had described contemporary society of France in a long series of novels and therefore his foreign imitators also tried to describe society in their countries in the form of the novel and at the same time to follow conscientiously the technique of their master and the principles which he had derived from natural science. He supplied no serviceable model, however, for the drama; his *Thérèse Raquin* was a failure as even his most enthusiastic partisans had to acknowledge.

The writers who wished to establish a naturalistic drama in Germany believed that they had found their master in the great Norwegian HENRIK IBSEN. This was an error, for Ibsen never wrote in naturalistic fashion in the sense in which Zola did. In his first drama, *Catilina,* he defined it as his purpose to represent the contradiction between will and possibility, between humanity and the individual; the tragedy and the comedy of humanity and of the individual conjointly was to be his drama.

At first he realized this purpose, treating preferably historical and legendary material with Romantic touch and in rhythmic form, but even in *The Comedy of Love* (1862) the action is laid in the present. With *The League of Youth* (1869) began the series of Ibsen's modern prose dramas. They all describe Norwegian society and show that its conditions, externally so well regulated, are in truth corroded with common selfishness, with prejudices and vices and are therefore not permanent.

The second of these plays, *The Pillars of Society* (1877), sums up this criticism in one great picture. The individual phenomena are then examined in *A*

Doll's House (1879) where, in the heroine Nora, is sketched the degeneration of the wife because of illiberal education and of unworthy society-position; also in *An Enemy of the People* (1882), which shows the harmful influence of public opinion, and in *Ghosts* (1883), a ruthless condemnation of modern marriage, based upon the laws of inheritance, the results of which come out in terrible form in the case of the wife who was bought, and of the offspring of the unnatural union. The *Wild Duck* (1884) forms the conclusion of this series. While Ibsen in the preceding dramas has everywhere defended the claims of truth and freedom and of the absolute assertion of individuality, he shows here the necessity of the society-lie and of dependence for the people of the present and seems to condemn his former endeavors as cruel and useless.

In the succeeding dramas he did not exercise any further criticism of society but made use of existing conditions only as a basis for the treatment of peculiar psychological problems. In *Rosmersholm* (1886) it is a question only of the fate of the individual so far as it depends on ethical principles. Even here there is an element of mysticism intermingled which next receives the principal attention in the *Lady from the Sea* (1888), a drama in which the psychological solution of the marriage question is attempted. In *Hedda Gabler* (1891) this element of the absolutely mysterious again disappears, though Hedda's condition has something entirely indefinable which conditions her state of feeling and the whole course of the action.

Then the mystical becomes dominant in *The Master Builder,* the tragedy of a will-power failing to act and in *Little Eyolf* (1894), a drama in which the impulse to evil is overcome and a selfish, sensual love is given up in favor of mighty deeds for the future. The last two works of Ibsen are variations of the same theme. In *John Gabriel Borckmann* (1896) and the sequel, *When We Dead Awaken* (1899), ruthless effort, even when it sets the highest aims before it, is attacked as a mortal enemy because it destroys the life of love, man's most valuable possession.

The error of the German naturalists, who believed that they saw in Ibsen an artist akin to Zola, arose from the fact that he, too, was unfriendly to embellishment, gave scenes from the life of the present, did not avoid the distasteful and employed the results of the modern natural sciences in the motivation and psychology of his dramas.

But all these new methods are in Ibsen at the service of the old problems of art which are no longer recognized by Naturalism. With their aid he desires to solve certain problems and to assign values. Not the simple connection of cause and effect but the sway of fate, though somewhat modern in dress, decides the result, which is specially conditioned by very complicated personalities. Because of this it loses the typical character required by Naturalism. And yet these personalities do not, as with earlier authors, stand in empty space; they must breathe the life of their times even if it is full of pestilence.

All this might also have been found in Hebbel's dramas, but Ibsen's technique appeared quite new and contributed most to his being reckoned among the Naturalists. Hebbel had made the implied demand that the spectator allow the validity of certain special conditions of the artistic world which are at variance with reality and himself aid the poet to this end by the display of a vigorous imagination. Ibsen, on the other hand, makes illusion easier than any of his predecessors. His characters speak as in real life; suggestively, brokenly, capriciously, revealing their thoughts only accidentally and unwillingly. Nothing seems to be said to instruct the hearers or to guide their judgment, but the consummate art of the dialogue produces an absolutely faithful picture of real conversation because the characters on the stage follow by inherent necessity the laws of the reciprocal interchange of thought. Moreover, we look deeper into their souls than was possible by the earlier method which only availed itself of conscious, pointed utterances on the stage. At the same time the events are imitated and joined to one another in a way which seems to have no regard at all for the spectator or the needs of dramatic construction and especially assists in producing the impression of a simple reproduction of an accidental event. In truth, however, there is to be recognized in this a triumph of the greatest command of dramatic art-form, for everything seemingly accidental is at the service of the problem of representing visibly the action in its course. True, Ibsen's idea of an action is different from that of the majority of his predecessors. He has gone deep in this way, that the outward action no longer dominates but the inward processes which condition and accompany the action are made perceptible to the senses. To demonstrate these as clearly as possible he makes the real action extremely limited and, like the Greek tragedians, represents on the stage only the final steps which lead to the fall. He is thus compelled to recover the earlier stages of the course of events in the form of an exposition which runs along through the whole play. In this he also shows in brilliant fashion his mastery over all devices by influencing his characters, without any visible compulsion but because of the given conditions, to communicate the necessary hypotheses.

By his enhancement of illusion, his deepening of the intellectual life and his perfect technique, Ibsen has become the most significant dramatist of the present day and no one who in seriousness writes for the stage can escape his influence, let him yield ever so reluctantly.

Ibsen's less important fellow-countryman, BJÖRN-STJERNE BJÖRNSON, has also made a strong impression in Germany and gained a certain influence. Even before Ibsen became known in Germany, *Ein Fallissement* (1874), a society-play made after French models but more realistic, had won its way on the stage and at the close of our period his double drama, *Über unsre Kraft* (1893-95), called forth passionate excitement. This, however, originated more from the religious subject of the first part and the social subject of the second than directly from the merit of the work. Björnson's technique always retains something of the conventional and the theatrical and cannot disown its descent from the French.

Björnson is still farther removed than Ibsen from Naturalism of which the Swede, AUGUST STRINDBERG, must be considered the most logical representative. In many of his dramas, such as *Der Vater* (1887), *Fräulein Julie* (1888), etc., he aims only at reproducing absolutely and faithfully from second to second in its outward course a scene from the world of reality and claims that to him the value and the influence of what is presented is quite indifferent. Of course this is in reality not the case and even with him there is not wanting a trend which, according to Naturalism, ought to be excluded.

Besides Ibsen and Strindberg there is a third nominally Naturalistic dramatist who acquired an influence in Germany, the Russian Count, LEO TOLSTOI. His really great drama, *The Powers of Darkness* (1887), throws a light upon the moral degradation of the Russian peasantry. Every one of their characteristics is faithfully noted and candidly reproduced but there is no effort to attain to the exactness demanded by Naturalism and the moral standard is not lacking. Rather, the purpose of the poet is directed to showing the connection between guilt and atonement in a dramatic action of the old style and, instead of scientific views, a fervent positive Christian conviction permeates the whole. Once again it is merely the psychological depth and the peculiar nature of the coarse incidents which ruthlessly reveal the depths of vice and contradict the old ideal of beauty that suggest the appearance of Naturalism.

On the basis of the impression produced by its foreign representatives in Germany, the essence of Naturalism is represented at the end of the eighties as follows: Naturalism chooses its material exclusively from the life of the present day and preferably from the domain of the lowly, the ugly and the morally objectionable, which up to the present has been excluded from artistic treatment. Instead of plots it offers accurately observed scenes and individual incidents which are to be considered typical of the conditions of society. In addition, abnormal morbid qualities are assigned to the characters introduced which, however, likewise claim a typical significance as the results of the unnatural conditions of modern life. Everything is derived from psychological and pathological causes. The law of causality holds unconditional sway, represented by scientific hypotheses, such as heredity and the influence of suggestion upon the will and by socialistic theories. Instead of strong utterances of passion, conversation alone serves as the means of sketching character and of disclosing the progress of events. Involuntary suggestions, instead of intentional communications, seeming equalization of what is essential and non-essential, avoidance of the monologue and of everything serving merely for the enlightenment of the spectator, and the most accurate prescriptions for everything external are to produce complete illusion without any assistance from the imagination of the spectator.

The single aim is ostensibly to do battle against lying, hypocrisy and whatever is antiquated in art and life. At the same time judgment is mostly given from the standpoint of youthful inexperience and of extreme political and social endeavor which would like at one stroke to put a new order of society and a new art in the place of the old, and to which therefore everything is welcome which makes light of prevailing views.

THE "FREE THEATRES"

From the year 1885 Naturalism has been a force in Germany in lyric poetry and in drama, and has been fostered by individual, mostly quite young authors. Although it had to encounter the most violent attacks from the moral, political and æsthetic point of view and its representatives were, in fact, haled before the courts to give answer for their faith, yet the new ideas gradually did, after all, make a place for themselves and gained enthusiastic admirers, especially among the young people of the large cities.

But all hope of winning over the regular theatres seemed excluded. They were surrounded, as it were, by a threefold wall, the anxious regard of their managers for all possible prejudices of middle-class society, the superficial love of amusement on the part of the public and the censorship of the police, which, devoid of all artistic judgment, forbade everything which seemed to contain a criticism of existing conditions or was not allowable in life, according to the judgment of the normal state-official, or indeed offended merely against æsthetic rules. The police, as everybody knows, have in Germany the office of defending against every attack, not only religion, custom and order, but even the taste of the citizens.

Under these circumstances the production of a naturalistic drama in Germany was, it seemed, impossible. But in Paris the actor Antoine had established a *théâtre libre,* which arranged performances for the members of a society only and therefore could not be troubled by police censorship and was not influenced by the "business" interest of the ordinary theatre.

After this model the *Freie Bühne* society of Berlin originated in April, 1889. In the choice of dramatic works, as well as in their presentation on the stage, its aim was to aspire to a *living* art uninfluenced by any reference to models or artistic perfection. Especially those dramas were to be considered which, because of their nature, were not acceptable to the regular theatres.

The Berlin "Free Theatre" began its activity in the autumn of 1889 with Ibsen's *Ghosts* and in the first year of its existence reached the goodly number of about 700 members. The half of the other plays it offered were translations: *Henrietta Maréchal,* by the brothers Goncourt, a finely conceived but ineffectively presented section of actual life; *Der Handschuh* by Björnson, a thesis-play, which, in spite of the importance of the problem, was likewise no gain to the stage; Tolstoi's *Powers of Darkness* and the unimportant play, *Auf dem Heimwege* by the Norwegian Alexander Kielland. German literature was represented by Fitger's *Von Gottes Gnaden,* a drama of the old style which had been refused entry to the stage merely from political timidity, by Anzengruber's *Viertes Gebot* and by three works of authors, up to that time unknown, who were faithfully following in the footsteps of French and Norwegian Naturalism: *Die Familie Selicke,* the joint production of Arno Holz and Johannes Schlaf, which presented indifferent events with painful tediousness, and the two maiden works of Gerhart Hauptmann.

For the first time attention was here called to the prominent figure of the Silesian dramatist and the violent conflict of opinions which his dramas caused gave significance to the important success which the Berlin "Free Theatre" gained during the brief period of its prime. What only individual productions from foreign countries had for a long time previously been able to do, that is, excite general and passionate interest in a work intended for the theatre, this a German author now succeeded in for the first time.

In the second year the Berlin "Free Theatre" was able to offer its members only five additional performances, among which, along with Hauptmann's *Einsame Menschen*, Otto Erich Hartleben's *Angèle* at most had a certain importance. In the third year there was only one single performance, Strindberg's *Komtesse Julie*. The board of directors explained that the mission of the "Free Theatre" was fulfilled. The real cause of the rapid decline was, however, the lack of available works of a naturalistic tendency.

The same fate befell the other societies which had been founded with the same purpose as the Berlin "Free Theatre" in Munich, Vienna, Leipzig, Dresden and other cities. In itself it was a happy idea for circles gifted with artistic taste to cut loose by their own inherent strength from the degenerate practices of the regular theatres, though Richard Wagner had already anticipated them in his Bayreuth "patronage society." The idea came to naught because the guiding spirits of the "Free Theatres" allowed themselves to be carried along exclusively by the current of Naturalism. The dangerous rocks on which their boat went to pieces were lack of dramatic interest and of æsthetic satisfaction in the plays presented. When the first curiosity had been satisfied, the majority of their adherents returned penitently to the old style.

And yet the "Free Theatres" had gained a valuable victory by their activity. The limits of the permissible were extended, new subjects had been introduced, a more faithful presentation of external and internal developments was recognized as a most important duty of the dramatist, careful observation took the place of conventional characterization and the technique of author and actor endeavored to arrive at complete illusion. At the same time a keener judgment revealed the worthlessness of the hollow forms and of the phrase-filled idealism of the decadent literature, of the but seemingly modern society-plays aiming at outward effect and of the silly comedy and degenerate folk-play with its regular conventional figures.

For some years it seemed as if the classic plays also, especially those of Schiller's last period, would be drawn down into this whirlpool, but the outlook soon cleared. It was recognized that these works had preserved their full life and power throughout the nineteenth century and that it was merely denied to the workers of an altogether differently constituted time to give true and complete expression to their thoughts and feelings with the same artistic means.

Those older dramatists who had endeavored to reach this goal, Hebbel, Ludwig and Anzengruber, only now secured a proper appreciation; the works of the mature Grillparzer, such as *Die Jüdin von Toledo* and *Libussa*, shone out with new brilliancy, and forgotten precursors of Naturalism, like Büchner, Dulk and Nierbergall were rediscovered. These earlier writers had also to make up for the lack of artistic and technically capable representatives of the "moderns."

It soon turned out that the attempt to establish an entirely new dramatic art in Germany had failed. The features peculiar to Naturalism that were of use were

now combined in milder form with the old subjects
and with the old technique by certain of its first partisans and new rising talents but without the pretense
of driving out the old art.

HERMANN SUDERMANN

While extreme Naturalism was undone because it was
unable to conjure up a new drama by magic, prudent
writers, acting as mediators between the old and the new,
chose well-beaten paths. In part they injected new
life into the old historical drama by weaving into it
realistic effective figures, as did Wildenbruch; in part
they anticipated the newly awakened interest in the
entire life of the present in that, while avoiding everything too offensive, they presented the proletariat and
the inferior creatures, who had been unnoticed before
or had appeared only in idealizing colors on the stage,
as well as characters from the higher and middle classes
who were now conceived of in a slightly less conventional fashion. In this they made careful use of the
expedients of naturalistic art but in general adhered
closely to the old well-connected plot and exercised all
other considerations for what was suitable to the stage.

In the same year that the Berlin "Free Theatre"
began its activity, the most successful representative
of this middle party, HERMANN SUDERMANN, was allowed, after long waiting, to bring his play, *Die Ehre*
(1889), upon the stage.

Unadjusted and unconnected, the old and the new art
are still found side by side. One-half of the play
belongs to the *Vorderhaus* and without any essential
changes the well known figures of German middle-class

plays come on the stage: the rich merchant prince, his vain gossiping wife, his frivolous spoiled son and the noble daughter who stands apart from the materialism of the rest of the family and cannot disavow her descent from Wallenstein's Thekla. She loves a poor but very virtuous youth and the subject of the plot, as with innumerable predecessors, is the overcoming of the difficulties which lie in the way of the union of the two. But while elsewhere the middle-class family appears alone upon the scene and the solution is brought about by some lucky accident, the saving of a life, an inheritance or some similar cheap expedient, Sudermann has given new charm to the old material by the introduction of a house in the court (*Hinterhaus*), that is, a lower class of society which with hatred and jealousy watches the rich house and endeavors to rise to its easier life, whether by honorable work or by vice. This proletariat had not as yet appeared upon the stage in its true form. Honest workmen were only allowed to show themselves in clean clothes and with clean language; common vice was represented only by comical, harmless drunkards or Magdalenes who were firmly convinced of the sinfulness of their doings. No dramatist had ventured to represent such characters in their true form and as a necessary product of the social conditions of the present. As in life so all the more on the stage, so-called good society tried to deny the existence of persons of this class or allowed them at most to put in an appearance in little episodes, in order to obtain certain piquant effects. On the other hand, Sudermann gave them equal dramatic rights and now when they appeared before the public in full life-size, they were looked at with a mixture of curious astonishment and disgust. Especially Alma Heinecke with her matter-of-course immorality was a stone of stumbling for all who wanted to see on the stage no vice but that which had been punished and reformed. But the low sentiments of her parents, of her sister Auguste and of the brother-in-law Michalski were, taken all in all, much more disgusting, because their cowardly cringing to the rich and their love of money and enjoyment came out in brutal ugliness, while Alma possessed at least the charm of youthful grace and naïveté.

With accurate judgment as to what it was possible to use on the stage, Sudermann has sketched this group and its environment, so that everywhere the individual traits contribute matter in confirmation of the scenes to which even in this play the chief interest is turned. At the same time a diverting effect is produced by the purposely exaggerated description of their vulgarity. There is no pretence of a profound characterization nor any intention of proving the rottenness of society conditions. The difference of the classes is rather employed merely to exemplify the theme under discussion. This theme, that every class has its own conception of honor, is proved by the course of the action, as in French society-plays, and is discussed by the *raissonneur,* a figure introduced expressly for this purpose, from a lofty standpoint and as wittily as possible. But, after all, it is a question merely of an entertaining play, in spite of the appearance of the more serious purpose of fathoming life's contradictions. This is clearly shown at the end where money, which before had been charged with the blame of all deterioration, now outwardly makes everything good, while in truth nothing has happened to reconcile the profound contrasts. Also in the conduct of the dialogue in the front-house scenes and in a plentiful use of clever ideas and surprising comparisons there is an imitation of French society-plays.

In this manner Sudermann was able with accurate choice to unite in his first play everything, both from old and new, that it seemed possible to turn to good account on the stage at that time and the most brilliant success attended his shrewd calculation, backed up, as it was, by an uncommonly strong theatrical talent. No German theatre, apart from some Court theatres which adhered to their principles, was able for long to resist the incentive of the proceeds promised by *Die Ehre*, or the longing of the public for its production, so that Sudermann plucked the first ripe fruit of the new efforts to establish a drama suitable to the times.

That this suitability did not agree with the real state of affairs, as far as the great majority of the public was concerned, Sudermann had to acknowledge when his second drama, *Sodoms Ende* (1891), was ruthlessly rejected by the same public which had applauded *Die Ehre*. In this play he has painted in much deeper and truer colors the same front-house which was described in *Die Ehre* in the customary kindly colors. Their moral rottenness, their coarse sensuality, their contempt for anything loftier than gain and enjoyment was shown without any toning down of its revolting nature. A young artist is dragged away from a modest happiness to his ruin by a lascivious woman of Berlin's financial circles and along with him a girl who had in vain endeavored to struggle upward out of the iridescent slough.

Granted that *Sodoms Ende* is not the equal of *Die*

Ehre in direct dramatic power, that was after all not
the reason of the failure, but the fact that the public
usually occupying the parquet and boxes likes to see
everything on the stage "without paint" except its
own picture.

Although in this play, too, the old-fashioned *raison-
neur* plies his trade, still Sudermann's second drama is
far more of a unit in style than his first.   The conditions
are described at length, the soul-life of the chief characters is made individual and is finely analyzed and the
course of the action develops logically from the preliminary conditions.   No theme is to be advanced and
proven, but a piece of life is given, in too personal a
conception, which generalizes too hastily the accidental
impressions of certain *parvenu* circles and yet without
any interference with their real life.   A few particulars,
such as especially the very sharp contrast of the artist's
home with the false brilliance into which he is drawn,
remind us of the author of *Die Ehre*.

The failure of *Sodoms Ende* made Sudermann more
careful.   In *Die Heimat* (1893) he reverted to his first
well-approved style of connecting an exciting action
with a description of present day conditions so that the
inherent contrasts come out in directly effective clashes.
While in *Sodoms Ende* he was a partisan, here he leaves
his own conception of people and events more in doubt.
By doing this he fulfils, it is true, a requirement of
Naturalism but takes from the drama the substance
of a basic idea.   The theme is very cleverly presented
so that a mild light falls on the old-fashioned society
with its limited view-points, its rigid but at the same
time firm and bracing ethics, its self-sacrificing spirit
and its modesty, while the newly gained freedom of the

individual who strives upward by his own effort is woven about with a gleaming splendor. In Magda, the representative of this new nature, he has created a captivating rôle and has besides scattered throughout the whole play such a great variety of striking external effects that he has given to the stage a work whose international success has only been attained, among all German dramas, by Kotzebue's *Menschenhass und Reue*.

But in this fact lies the proof also that the inherent import, which can be easily comprehended by any class of public of any nation, is not so very deep. In this play it is of course not a question of great and general human relations but of such as grow out of the life of specifically unimportant people of the present day in Germany. At the same time, however, the almost unexampled success of *Die Heimat* furnished proof that conscientious observance of reality and its reproduction with a proper adaptation to the conditions of stage effect afford the means of charming large audiences and that without transgressing against the nature of art. Therefore one ought not to condemn this middle class, to which *Die Heimat* belongs, so disdainfully as often happens.

Once more Sudermann attempted to picture a definite social class in *Die Schmetterlingsschlacht* (1893) and at the same time allowed accurate calculation of the external factors of the action to drop into the background; once more the result was at first rejection, which later indeed gave way to kindly and continued applause because of growing recognition of the good properties of the play. Repentantly Sudermann bowed to the wish of his public and from now on was submissive. All grand and bold desires, all artistic purposes were permitted to hold sway only as long as the prevailing taste and the external effect conditioned by it was not prohibited. Only in one single instance, when a lucky chance did not demand the intervention of this highest court, did he succeed in another work of fine quality. The one-act play, *Fritzchen,* inserted in an otherwise unimportant cycle of one-act plays, *Morituri* (1897), shows how an effeminate young fellow, through lack of firm grip and because of the rigidity of the idea of ''honor,'' is ruined in the enforced calling of officer, when he might have found happiness in a quiet everyday life. The incident, and the environment as well, is comprehended in its deepest import and worked out very effectively with a few strokes, the emotional effect being always kept in view.

All the rest of Sudermann's dramas after *Die Schmetterlingsschlacht* are plays aiming at effect. The first of them, *Das Glück im Winkel* (1895), avoids at the end, with difficulty and in an improbable manner, the same conflict that is carried through logically to its tragic issue in *Fritzchen.* It aims at awakening the belief that, for the gentle husband whom a brutal hand has torn from his dream of happiness and for the wife who has destroyed their married life, companionship is still possible on the ruins of their partnership.

After the failure of Naturalism, when the historical problem-drama seemed to be the order of the day, Sudermann tried in *Johannes* (1898), with insufficient powers, to depict the portentous times before the appearance of Christ and to place the hero between the setting and the new rising world. For the decadent representatives of a depraved and decayed antique culture he could effectively employ the colors from *Sodoms*

Ende, but he did not succeed in entering into an appreciation of the prophetic childhood of developing Christendom, so that the reflection of the blood-red sinking sun of the ancient world and of the gently rising mild constellation of the new produced only an unsteady flickering. The effort to combine the description of the inherent contrast of two ages with the accumulated external impressions, which seem to Sudermann indispensable, resulted in a mixture which possibly might dazzle at the moment but must soon be recognized as inartistic and immoral.

The *Drei Reiherfedern* (1898) is just as confused, and again attempted unsuccessfully to entice the spectator into a distant world. Because the present seemed to long to get back to the mysterious fairy-world of Romanticism, Sudermann now offered a fairy-play, intermingled with symbolical elements, but this domain was sealed to the clear-headed poet. He quickly turned his back upon it and directed himself to the present, which by the way, is the real theatre of his work.

The great and principal question of the present is how the primitive instincts or the freedom won by conscious will power have to be correlated to the narrow forms safeguarded by reverence and the rigid traditional ethics of society. This becomes the chief interest in his following works. While in the more meritorious *Johannisfeuer* (1899) the innate power of the impulses is destroyed in the conflict with the prevailing view of life, *Es lebe· das Leben* (1902) makes the desire for happiness felt by the more gifted character conclude a compromise with Society and its ethics which brings blessing to him and to others. The love of the wife who, with a not improbable cleverness, succeeds in finding this tortuous road to what was in her judgment a worthy existence, elevates the man of her heart and they both stand on the heights of a ripe art of living, after they have conquered their passions. By a blind chance the secret of their intimacy is discovered and the wife sacrifices herself instead of the lover.

Sturmgeselle Sokrates (1903) belongs again to the plays not rare with Sudermann which terminate without any profit, for the reason that a fine original thought is made coarse and distorted in the straining after rude effects. Certainly a gentle hand could have made a warm, cheerful and touching figure of the man of forty-eight years whose ideals had become inelastic. So also in *Stein unter Steinen* (1903) there was no need of making merely a melodramatic theatrical figure out of the noble murderer Biegler who, after his release from the reformatory, has to suffer so grievously from the prejudices of the members of his guild. How well Anzengruber knew how to get at the bottom of a similar motive in *Fleck auf der Ehr'!* But the necessary courage in quest of truth in such problems is rarely in accord with the taste of the public and there result those incredible conclusions which do violence to all finer artistic feelings and which, by a fortunate turn, dragged in by main force, open up the prospect of the happy solution so indispensable to the superficial perceptions of the average public.

When a man of great talents like Sudermann condescends to such expedients, he certainly does not do it voluntarily and the fault lies more with the low condition of artistic taste than with him. And further, what in him is criticized severely as an unpardonable moral defect, has been at all times an accompaniment

of creative work for the stage, just as it has been impossible for writers with the greatest gifts to carry
out their great purposes in defiance of the public.   In
this they have scarcely ever succeeded directly, or have
been unable to combine genuine artistic power with a
regard for the taste of the times, which none of the
great ones have ever lost sight of, neither Shakespeare,
nor Molière, nor Schiller.   If only an author does not
condescend to flatter the likings of the public which
are contrary to the rules of art, if only a sound germ
and an honest striving after truth is not lacking in
his works, it is not permissible to deny them the rank
of works of art solely because of a shrewd calculation
on popular effect.   To be sure, the mightiest dramatic
talents succeed in combining the unconscious with this
reasonable calculation, so that their works appear as
the products of an inward compulsion uninfluenced by
any regard for externals, but these perfect dramas are
too rare to supply the daily needs of the stage.   Sudermann deserves commendation that he alone of all living
authors understands how to satisfy this need with the
greatest technical skill.

PLAYWRIGHTS OF THE PRESENT DAY

There is in German literary circles a small but powerful party which condemns unconditionally, as treachery
to art, any compromise with traditional forms, or any
yielding to the desire of the public for theatrical effect.
To these critics Sudermann, the most successful of the
stage writers of the present day, is most distasteful
and every one of his works on its appearance is attacked
by them with the greater virulence, the greater its

success has been. They condemn his "manufacture" unconditionally, but justly only when he places it at the service of low ideals. His theatrical ability and accurate technique are certainly no fault. And yet it often has the appearance as if in it, in and for itself, there were something objectionable. The contempt for outward form, peculiar to the Germans, which has robbed so many of their best writers of success on the stage, easily conduces to the idea of seeing something ignoble or undignified and speculative in its possession. There is really no occasion whatever for this judgment.

Such kindly pleasant pictures as ERNST WICHERT offered to the public in a long series are surely not hurtful food. His dramatic writings began as early as 1858 and especially in the field of the finer comedy he obtained charming effects, as in *Ein Schritt vom Wege* (1871), *Der Freund des Fürsten* (1879) and *Post Festum* (1890). ADOLF WILBRANDT, in his *Meister von Palmyra* (1889), produced a thought-drama beautiful in form and very successful in spite of its undramatic structure. He provided light entertainment without any serious purpose in his fine comedy, *Der Unterstaatssekretär* (1891).

This is really the field in which LUDWIG FULDA's charming talents are well displayed. With a comedy in verse, *Die Aufrichtigen* (1883), he first showed his unusual cleverness in form, which since then has risen to genius, especially in his translation of Molière's chief works (1892) and of Rostand's fine comedies, such as *Les Romanesques* (1895) and *Cyrano de Bergerac* (1898). The graceful but too very hastily sketched plays, *Die Zwillingsschwester* (1900) and *Novella d'*

Andrea (1903), also prove this.   When he tries to give
form to serious conditions of the times or even to write
historical tragedies, as in *Das verlorene Paradies* (1890),
Die Sklavin (1891), *Herostrat* (1898) and *Maskerade*
(1904), his powers fail him.   For the fairy-drama his
inventive imagination is also insufficient and in vain
does he try to cover up the lack of it by neat witticisms
and brillant form.   In spite of this the dramatic fairy
story, *Der Talisman* (1892), was the most successful
of his works because it came out just when Naturalism
had awakened a great longing for charm and depth of
thought.   A certain reality also contributed to the great
success which far surpassed the real worth of the play.
With later works of a similar nature Fulda could gain
no influence, while his comedies, *Die Kameraden* (1894),
Jugendfreunde (1897), were as before greeted with applause whenever they were not altogether too lacking
in substance as was *Kaltwasser* (1902).   FRIEDRICH
ADLER also deserves mention as a clever versifier and
adapter of Spanish comedies, as *Zwei Eisen im Feuer*
(1900) after Calderon and *Don Gil* (1902) after "Tirso
de Molina."

The dramatists who make use of the life of the
present for theatrical effect in serious and light comedy
are strongly influenced by the desire for a faithful reproduction of reality.   Such are HERMANN FABER-
GOLDSCHMIDT in *Ewige Liebe* (1897) and *Frau Lili*
(1902) and GEORG ENGEL in *Die goldene Lüge* (1892),
Über den Wassern (1901) and *Im Hafen* (1904).   But
these authors are altogether too lacking in the captivating power of original talent for the stage and this
prevents their purpose of influencing the public by
an outwardly effective treatment of the serious problems

of the times from being crowned with any great show
of success.

What these latter lack, FELIX PHILIPPI possesses without doubt in the highest degree.   He knows exactly all
the expedients, great and small, with which the appearance of an action can be imposed upon an audience
and the feelings of the great mass stirred up and he
makes use, without any artistic scruple, of the vulgar
interest in the most recent events of the day, or of
curiosity, to get a glance behind the scenes of contemporary history.   By transferring his "actual" materials to another sphere, from the political to the
industrial for example, he disguises the facts and characters he employs only so lightly that a cursory glance
penetrates the mask.   At the central point he puts some
sort of stage-effect that will shock the strongest nerves
and in this way produces an excitement which, because
the heart is never touched, is felt as a pleasant charm
by those who seek only entertainment from the stage.
This excitement, however, has nothing in common with
any kind of artistic effect.

With still greater success OTTO ERNEST (-SCHMIDT) has
trodden the road to sure royalties, when in his *Jugend
von heute* (1899), which gave itself in addition some
airs of literary authority, he helped Philistinism to
victory over the "moderns" who, in distorted pictures,
were given over to ridicule.   In this play, as in his far
weaker comedies, *Flachsmann als Erzieher* (1901),
Gerechtigkeit (1902) and *Bannermann* (1904) a "purpose" was intended to replace the insufficient dramatic
ability of the otherwise so unerring and well-balanced
author.   The first two attempts succeeded indeed be-

cause of a clever choice of theme, but in the end these untruthful exaggerations will not maintain their hold especially as they are translated so clumsily into action.

The comedies not related to any time may hope for a longer period of life, as they are merely to amuse, whether by historical anecdotes as in *Wie die Alten sungen* (1895) by CARL NIEMANN, or by a sort of local coloring, as in the comedies of RICHARD SKOWRONNEK, *Halali, Die stille Wache* and *Waterkant* (1904). In these everything depends upon discovering a hitherto unworked field which appeals to the great public and by its new charms bribing the judgment. Most successfully was this managed by WILHELM MEYER-FÖRSTER with the dramatized novel, *Alt Heidelberg* (1898), which compounded sentimentality and Heidelberg student-life, crowned with its halo of poetry, to make the very tastiest theatrical mixture; also by ARNO HOLZ, aided by OSWALD JERSCHKE, in the high school play, *Traumulus* (1904).

In this mixture there was still lacking two ingredients to drive out even the last thought of any artistic purpose: the comic of situation at all costs and empty play on words, both of which aim merely at exciting peals of laughter. Wherever they hold sway, all regard for a connected plot and for characterization vanishes, all trace of an idea is lacking and at most the semblance of proper feelings is awakened by the aid of false sentimentality. In regard to such a play, whoever ventures to raise even the most modest claims to good taste is laughed out of court by the author who carries on his writing according to principles of the unscrupulous merchant and like him has only gain in view. This class of plays occupies the chief place on the German stage to judge from the number of times they are acted and their typical representative is OSKAR BLUMENTHAL.

At the beginning of his career he pursued more serious purposes: his comedies, *Der Probepfeil* (1882) and *Die grosse Glocke* (1883), his drama, *Ein Tropfen Gift* (1885) could still rank as carefully executed, entertaining and exciting society-plays, although everything in them was already made subject to theatrical effect. But later Blumenthal kept lowering his aim. He now carried on the business usually with the actor Kadelburg, and with their farce, *Im weissen Ross'l* (1898), the two reached a total of performances never before equalled. Kadelburg was an advisor who knew the stage and had even earlier been connected with the humorist FRANZ VON SCHÖNTHAN in *Die berühmte Frau* (1887), *Zwei glückliche Tage* (1893) and *Der Herr Senator* (1894). Schönthan further "composed" with GUSTAV VON MOSER a number of farces, such as *Krieg im Frieden* (1879), and with his brother Paul, *Der Raub der Sabinerinnen* (1878), which, because of the Saxon dialect of a strolling director and a rich collection of stage anecdotes, created extraordinary amusement. Then when, after the stormy days of Naturalism, the gracious morn of poetry seemed about to dawn, Schönthan modernized, with Koppel-Ellfeld, the historical comedy in verse, so popular at the beginning of the century, such as *Komtesse Guckerl* (1895), *Renaissance* (1896), *Die goldene Eva* (1896), by dressing up in the clothes of earlier days and in gayer colors the customary figures and situations of the modern farce. This proceeding was also imitated by Blumenthal with success in *Der Schwur der Treue*

(1905), when he found that the old-fashioned farces were no longer drawing well.

Other double firms, like Laufs and Jacoby, Walther and Stein, competed with the above-named and likewise gathered in large sums. They delivered factory-work without any stamp of personality, calculated for whole-sale consumption. All questions of the times were anxiously avoided so as not to excite offence in any listener; all higher interests had to be excluded, merely of course to restrain the spectators from reflection and even the coarsest expedients were not disdained if they had power to excite laughter. As compared with these plays even Kotzebue's slight comedies are still to be called works of art because in them there is to be found at least superficial characterization and a plot according to a definite plan. Likewise the French farces, justly condemned so severely and so lacking in morality, far surpass the clumsy German "manufactures," which like them aim at amusing, by their careful work, their sur-prising inventions and easy even if frivolous charm. England alone has furnished something similar in its stupid farces (e. g. *Charley's Aunt* by Thomas) with their circus humor which is also applauded in Germany.

But even these do not touch the lowest point of stage productions in the present day. This is found in the degenerate Berlin farce and the Vienna operetta where the disgusting exhibition of naked women is joined to the other absurdities.

These products of the most vulgar scheming do not concern the history of dramatic literature but they must be mentioned so as to characterize the low condition of taste at the very centres of intellectual life. For only when one with disgust takes them into consideration

does one recognize the hindrances which stand in the
way of all effort to maintain the old and to create a new
drama of a nobler kind.

LITERARY TENDENCIES IN PRESENT DAY DRAMA

Under the designation "literary" are summed up
at the present time all those efforts which aim to advance
literature in its artistic creative work but which are
free from outward regard for the inclinations of the
public, and free from the constraint of tradition. This
point of view is the only common one from which, in a
summary of the drama of the present day, valuable and
independent beginnings and productions are distinguished from the great mass of stage-plays.

The time is not yet ripe for an historical review
of the development of the drama during the last decade
of the nineteenth century. There are too many pro-
miscuous and uncertain movements and a temporary
disappearance or a sudden rise does not in any way
betoken the final destiny of any one of the many classes.
Besides, almost all dramatists of these later times have
made trial one after another of the most widely different, often diametrically opposite styles, so that the colors
under which the individual writers appear are for the
most part as varied as the whole picture.

In this there are prominent at first in the beginning
of the nineties the efforts of the extreme Naturalists
who were, however, not able to get a secure footing
on the stage. From about 1892 the scientific and socialistic basic view-points of Naturalism were replaced by
the enthusiastic reception of the aristocratic teaching

of the poet-philosopher Friedrich Nietzsche. In another place * I have endeavored to paraphrase the nature of this in the following words: "Nietzsche is enthusiastic for beauty and sees in the masses merely the tools of the great. The duty of mankind according to him is to produce unique great men, philosophers, artists, saints. In his book, *Also Sprach Zarathustra* (1883–92), he develops his teaching in regard to the superman, in which the species appears on a higher plane of development or the individual raises the species to his level. According to this the superman arises by cultivation or by chance at the close of a long ascending period of development. As lawgiver and inventor he creates new ideals in all fields and opposes to the old Christian, liberal and social values others by which is guaranteed to the individual the development of all his powers in freedom and beauty. Nietzsche does not, however, end up in anarchy, but in aristocracy, for he gives to the strong the right to rule the weak and the low.

In this teaching there was so much that agrees with Egoism and the noble desire for individual freedom and it was offered in such a seductive dress that the youth became enthusiastic and applauded Nietzsche though without understanding. People had for so long believed in the unconditional authority of law in all departments of life and been oppressed by it and the ugly had only just finished celebrating its orgies when Zarathustra appeared as a deliverer. The wonderful language in its prophetic speeches, its symbolism and aphorisms incited even to superficial imitation and the great

* In Spemann's *Das goldene Buch der Weltliteratur.* (L. E. H.)

thought of a new world of heroic beings soon took root. Everyone who was unwilling to set bounds to his actions and thoughts believed that he might consider himself a superman, if he only played the strong man, set regard for others aside and made an outward boast of superior refinement in spite of rudeness of heart.

It belongs to the nature of the "upland man" that he should despise the lowlands of life with its everyday bustle and its dirt, its joys and sorrows, all too modest for him. He either lives out his own life in the ruthless egoism of the "all-round" man of the Renaissance and employs in all directions the surplus of his mental and bodily powers, while unsparingly trampling underfoot everything that is sacred to others or he cherishes only in his heart great thoughts which do not develop into practical knowledge but through his artistic work come to light in dark mysterious symbols as hazily as they dawn upon himself.

The magnificent metaphors and the self-created style of Nietzsche offered the material for this symbolism, which is filled with a longing for the unknown, and with the feeling of the great mystic unity of the unconscious in man and in nature.

To the symbolists this uncertain groping in the night-regions of the soul seems far more valuable than the bright daylight of reasonable conduct. Complete and passive surrender to a world of dreams they consider the only method of artistic creation and enjoyment. Their conception of art comes in touch with that of the Romanticists at the beginning of the century which was likewise swayed by the loftiest subjectivity and a longing for a comprehension of the unconscious.

"New Romanticism" has developed out of Symbolism

since about 1895 and again its favorite field for subjects is the fairy-story. Its aim is to combine, as in Novalis and Tieck, naïveté and lofty symbolism, direct expression of the deepest feelings and weighty thought, contempt for the age and an ideal picture of a genuine and loftier humanity.

The acquisitions of psychological science in the nineteenth century anticipate this combination of the most varied objects because it is, after all, mere self-revelation on the basis of a keen dissection of one's own inner life. At the same time these New Romanticists derive advantage from the better aids for the suggestion of artistic impressions which the technique of the Naturalists has produced.

They, too, aim at giving pictures and despise dramatic art of the older style. But while Naturalism at least offered reality in its palpable brutality, here everything dissolves into airy floating creations and only a superfine feeling can follow up all the emotions of the poets in their spirit-like utterances. Therefore this aristocratic, profound art which surpasses all earlier technique, is limited by its nature to a quite narrow circle. Its creations cannot possibly foreshadow the drama of the future.

It would seem that for the present they are the last stage by way of attempts to create a new drama without any regard to tradition. And yet the circle of possibilities is unlimited and who can say whether the near future will not produce a literature which will solve the problem of giving to the present its own peculiar style of art.

To-day, indeed, in place of the pleasurable anticipation which prevailed ten years ago, the spirit of resigna-

tion seems to have come. The works of Shakespeare,
Goethe, Šchiller and Grillparzer are once more plainly
in the foreground. Desire for the impression of suitability to the times has ceased, the historical drama and
the problem-play are celebrating their resurrection in
purified form. The dramatic art of which Joseph Kainz
is now the greatest representative is purifying and
supplementing in a modern sense the characters of the
great plays of the past by covering the outlines marked
out by the poet with the transparent colors of unconscious, nervous moods. To be sure, this disturbs a part
of the clear plastic of these works of art but, as a
recompense, it creates new charms more acceptable to
the sentiment of the present day.

At the same time this combination is after all but
a makeshift towards getting over the lack of living
modern dramas. The classic drama demands that it
be played and felt in the spirit of its time and besides,
we are still able to enjoy it. It has not lost its ethical
and artistic effect, indeed its value is to be estimated
higher than formerly, because it offers a perfected form
and a developed style, just what the present lacks. The
absence of those lately acquired technical art-devices,
which produce complete illusion without any effort on
the part of the spectator, is rather to be called an advantage in so far as the imagination is spurred on to
great activity and the incitements having the strongest
effect on the stage, viz: interest in the plot and the
characters and the contents of thought and feeling,
are not encroached upon and weakened by indifferent
externals and excessively refined moods.

The theatre comes only into consideration as a directly
influential factor of elevating pleasure and of higher

education in so far as it finds ready in the thought and feelings of the spectator a ground capable of receiving its gifts. Although the new forms offer to the artistically refined spirit greater satisfaction, though the profounder heart-life and the more impressionable feelings mean, as they doubtless do, a valuable acquisition, so long as the understanding of the works produced by their aid is limited to such small circles as has hitherto been the case, they must not presume to despise the older art, as if it were worthless. To measure works of art by the standard of suitability to the times is evidence of a lack of culture and of the historic sense. Art fulfils its lofty mission only when it brings us out of the narrow circle of our own limited existence into its boundless and timeless dominion where we forget life and its limitations and by sympathy are absorbed in the poetic production whether its outer form be borrowed from a past century or from the present.

In contrast with the Decadence which, interested for so long in a one-sided culture of beauty, had lost all connection with the life of the present, Art now recognizes that its chief mission is to give form to the ideas which hold sway in its own time and so serve truth and beauty at the same time. It must therefore keep its finger on the pulse of its times. But where is the beat to be felt most distinctly? The majority thinks at the centres of public life with their increased sensitiveness, their flooding life, their authoritative influences in so many directions. However, the man who considers the Germany of to-day dispassionately sees that the cities, which have grown so rapidly to an immense size, do not represent German nature, that in them views prevail which are modified by international influence or else certain lines of German character are peculiarly exaggerated and twisted. The drama especially cannot become a great popular factor if it follows the nervous movements of the life of a large city. It must go down deep into the soul of the people to find out what influences them and what they desire. This simple knowledge has been obscured by the fact that the chief cities, especially Berlin, Vienna and Munich, have now become the depots of artistic work. Writers imagine they hear the moving of the spirit of the times when they catch the notes of the asphalted streets and suppose that this combination of the hurry for gain and of the desire for sensation means a new and loftier step in national development.

To-day that is fortunately not yet true but the mistake is comprehensible and continually being confirmed because the mass of energy collected in the metropolitan cities seemingly places the rest of Germany in subjection and it is continually increased by the attraction which it exercises on all progressive elements.

Especially in the field of dramatic creation and of theatrical life this tendency is most clearly noticeable. If one were to judge according to the plays which have been given most frequently in these latter years, one would come to the conclusion that the culture of the large cities had repressed every peculiarity of the German races, all traditional customs and morality and put in their place a ruthless assertion of individuality unhindered by reverence and religion or the ability to react on all external impressions. But this conclusion is false. In the "provinces," as the *litterateurs* of Berlin by preference slightingly call the rest of Germany, the reflections of perverted metropolitan life are, with low curiosity or ignorant admiration, considered something strange. They mislead indeed the artistic and moral judgment, but they find no echo in the feelings of the spectators to whom Schiller's works still continue to mean what is loftiest and to whom the comedies of Benedix unfortunately appear far more congenial and entertaining than *Der Biberpelz*.

DRAMATIC WRITERS OF TO-DAY

From what has been said it follows that the dramatists who now are striving to solve new problems with new means are all to be considered as precursors, just as the "Storm and Stress" writers of the eighteenth century preceded the classic writers. Goethe and Schiller succeeded at that time in working out to a clear vision while their comrades wasted their powers in vain effort. So, too, on the literary battle-fields of to-day, so many hopeful and talented writers have already fruitlessly dissipated their energies, while of the survivors not one has as yet brought home the crown of victory.

The brief onset of Naturalism claimed the greatest number of victims. GERHART HAUPTMANN, the prominent leader, remained unscathed. At his side fought WILHELM WEIGAND in *Der Vater* (1894), and later delineated in masterly style the mighty lordly men of the *Cinque-cento*, as in *Lorenzino* (1897) and *Die Renaissance* (1899); also the youthful GEORG HIRSCHFELD, who squandered his talent for accurate observation and description, shown in the one-act play, *Zu Hause* (1895), on the correct reproduction of the ugly without any other end in view and remained longest true to the old flag of Naturalism, as in *Die Mütter* (1896), *Agnes*

Jordan (1898), *Pauline* (1899) and *Nebeneinander* (1904). He lacks the ability to combine his individual impressions into larger scenes and to breathe into them the power of independent life. For a time he attempted, but unsuccessfully, to cross over to the popular fairy-drama in *Der Weg zum Licht* (1902) and last tried his hand at comedy in *Spätfrühling* (1906), also without success.

On the other side of Hauptmann stood MAX HALBE. In *Die Jugend* (1893) he took the subject of the first sudden development of the sexual impulses. He had thus chosen a subject than which none could be more favorable for impressionist reproduction. Into a single moment is crowded the development of the suddenly growing passionate feelings and what seems new in every single case is in truth a typical incident in the truest sense arising from the most primitive impulses. Halbe made also a happy hit in that he placed the lovers in the simplest environment and did not obscure the developments of the physical life by any conditions of higher culture. Her surrender to over-powering impulses brought the girl, who is sketched with charming freshness and without any false naïveté, to the inevitable conflict with her innate moral ideas which had been strengthened by training and her lot in life and the idyll becomes an inexorable tragic fate. Even those who took a negative position in regard to Naturalism were deeply moved by his drama.

Never after did Halbe make a like impression. Through his comedy, *Der Walpurgistag* (1902), there befell him the fate of the poet Ansgar whose one single capture of the prize of victory became his ruin. He tried his hand without success at the rhymed comic play, *Der Amerikafahrer* (1904), or aimed at making the mighty power of a superman credible in *Der Eroberer* (1899). To the heartfelt description of an invigorating home-sickness in *Mutter Erde* (1897) his warm and honorable nature could give faithful but not dramatic expression and *Der Strom* (1903), the shallow but clever revision of the older *Eisgang,* can not be compared with *Die Jugend.*

An amusing but likewise undramatic description of those literary circles in which Naturalism was first cultivated was given by Ernst von Wolzogen in his comedy, *Das Lumpengesindel* (1892). The cheery wretchedness gave origin to a series of diverting and touching pictures of conditions, but again there was a lack of everything that would make a perfect work of art or satisfy the most modest demands of a specifically dramatic nature.

OTTO ERICH HARTLEBEN also possessed genuine humor. The youthful impudence of students sets its mark on the most of his stories, while with greater adaptability than the most of the Naturalists he succeeded in putting effectively on the stage the modern people of the large city as in *Angèle* (1891) and *Hanna Jagert* (1893). The little comedy, *Die sittliche Forderung,* was a capital and intrinsically very true parody of Sudermann's *Heimat,* but in his most successful work, *Rosenmontag* (1901), he has evidently become a follower. According to the well-tried recipe he has combined in this work outwardly faithful descriptions from the life of a certain circle—here the officer's world—with complaisancy to the demands of the public. In the episodes his extraordinary humorous talent is again shown.

With genuine humor but without dramatic **power**

JOSEF RUEDERER succeeded in depicting a very diverting episode of Bavarian country-life in his comedy, *Die Fahnenweihe* (1894). LUDWIG THOMA drew from the same soil stronger satirical effects in his *Lokalbahn* (1902).

Without such decided individuality as the preceding a number of additional authors have with naturalistic devices sketched for the stage their pictures of conditions. Some count only on the charm of the faithful description of some place in the lowlands of life and approximate the folk-play, the subjects of which they treat less considerately and with finer description of the emotions, as for instance JOHANNES SCHLAF in *Meister Ölze* (1892). In contrast to him, the Vienna writers FELIX DÖRMANN (really Biedermann) in *Ledige Leute* and PHILIP LANGMANN in *Bartel Turaser* (1897) do not at all disdain the coarse excitement of strong effects and melodrama.

The primitive power of the impulses, undiminished by any of the external forms which had made Anzengruber prefer country conditions, often attracts the dramatists of the present day also to describe them and yet there is left a general impression of repulsive ugliness and of lack of dramatic life, as in the plays by Gerhart Hauptmann's brother Carl, *Waldleute* (1895) and *Ephraims Breite* (1898). Like Gerhart he also did sacrifice to the modern drama of moods in *Marianne* (1894), to the symbolistic verse-drama in *Die Bergschmiede* (1904) and to the elegantly written peasant comedy in *Die Austreibung* (1905), always however without success.

The dramatists are more numerous who describe by preference the degenerate instincts, the diseased and decrepit will of the educated man of culture. In these the external world is no longer of chief importance.

It gives only the preliminary conditions for the distracted feelings, the representation of which is an end in itself and for which the Italian, Gabriel D'Annunzio, first gave the model by his richly colored descriptions of sensuous conditions. He combines real formative powers with a highly poetic and characteristic language which brings even the most foreign subject, surrounded by the magic of mysterious symbolism, near to his hearers by the influence of suggestion.

The Lyric poet, RICHARD DEHMEL, had a like aim in his tragedy, *Der Mitmensch* (1895), which was a total failure. In it he described the sufferings of the mediocre, slavishly devoted brother of the ideal superman and the society opposing them, which is distorted even to caricature. ERNST ROSMER (Elsa Porges) brings on the stage with modern technique in *Dämmerung* (1895) the old melodramatic figures of the noble artist misjudged by the world, the spoiled headstrong girl and the intellectual sacrificing wife, only that now the spoiled girl has studied medicine, the misjudged artist is a pioneer in Wagner music and the sacrificing wife hysterical, while instead of being laid in an ivy bower the scene is in a darkened sickroom. Afterwards the authoress made a more successful attempt in the fairy-play, *Königskinder* (1898), but was not able to create a living drama in her slender *Johannes Herkner* (1904).

MAX DREYER, on the other hand, showed his stage-skill even in his first play, *Drei* (1892), in which he treated feelingly and tenderly the conflict between love and friendship. Later, with repression of all higher artistic claims, he gave his talent full course in *In Behandlung* (1897), *Grossmama* (1898) and *Liebesträume* (1898). And yet there is not to be recognized in these the cool scheming of the practical stage-writers, eager for success but rather that fresh, naïve creation which gives something suitable to all his figures, even if *Der Probekandidat* (1899) borders on that business-like writing with a purpose which Otto Ernst pursues. With *Die Siebzehnjährigen* (1904) he returned to the serious dramatic work of his promising beginning.

A peculiarly uncertain character is HERMANN BAHR. At first a fully persuaded Naturalist who did not shrink from the most disgusting phenomena, as in *Die grosse Sünde* (1899) and in *Die Mutter* (1890), he followed all the changes of most recent times. The last stage he has up to the present reached is the Vienna society-play, such as *Der Star* (1898), *Wienerinnen* (1900), *Der Meister* (1903), a most unsuccessful description of an unscrupulous lordly fellow, and *Die Andere* (1905), the story of a mysterious girl with two souls. The easy pliancy of his artistic tastes is peculiar, too, to his women characters and over all his plays there lies the superfine sensuousness of the æsthete.

This quality is coupled with great technical skill in the most successful of the Vienna dramatists of to-day, ARTHUR SCHNITZLER. In his first work, *Anatol* (1893), the dramatic form is only an excuse to string together an amusing series of momentary pictures from the life of a worldling, but *Liebelei* (1895), and especially the one-act play, *Der grüne Kakadu* (1899), shows that the plastic formative power and energy of the genuine dramatist is not lacking and that he knows how to combine these with the different moods which are to him the most essential. There is in him the gentle ease of old Vienna and the frivolity of the modern large city, intimately joined because they both have had their final origin in the same unchanging folk-character. That with this there may be combined a certain seriousness, even if not very deep, is seen in Schnitzler's good play, *Der einsame Weg* (1904).

Where, however, the frivolous temper to which nothing is sacred is the sole guide without the addition of the lightly sentimental coloring of the old style, then the result is a limitless contempt for the world which seeks to crush even one's own personality with scorn and raillery. That is the real gist of the peculiarly attractive plays by FRANZ WEDEKIND such as *Frühlingserwachen* (1894), *Der Erdgeist* (1895) and *Der Kammersänger* (1899). His is a completely vicious nature, at the same time artistic through and through, driven from desire to enjoyment and in enjoyment languishing with desire, despising himself just as much as he does those who think they find in his work any lofty aim whatever. The omission of all reference to the supernatural and the conception and use of existence as of a mere given fact, is shown in its last artistic consequences in a horrifying manner in Wedekind's writings.

What can still produce a certain satisfaction in the Naturalistic authors who make only a superficial examination of phenomena, is a source of despair to the man who looks into the depths of his own soul and finds there nothing but emptiness. To escape this fate, more serious natures, who no longer shared the faith in the old ethical and metaphysical values, eagerly seized upon the compensation which seemed to be offered in mysticism, myth and fairy-story. They have put the blue flower in their coat of arms and sought the path which leads to the enchanted forest of fancy. But only a few

found it and the rest contented themselves with the
scenes in which once upon a time the Romanticists had
given expression to their feelings, full of presentiments
and overspread with wavering moonlight, or they followed the sweet, shuddering notes which the Belgian
MAURICE MAETERLINCK gave forth. Colors and tone-
effects, suggestions instead of clear expression, retarding
delay at the moment of greatest excitement, plain inter-
meddling on the part of supernatural powers, the same
expedients which Novalis, Tieck, Eichendorff, Zacharias
Werner and their successors employed, this present day
art also uses, only that now excessively refined, morbidly
excited nerves are made to tingle and listeners of like
nature are expected.

Maeterlinck planned a number of his early dramas
for the puppet-theatre, in order in this way to transfer
the scenes into the region of the fairy-story and of
childlike instinctive feeling. He has recourse to the
imagination and the unconscious recalling of incidents,
but reflection and strong willed passion are excluded.
It is a matter of indifference whether he takes his material from the domain of the fairy-story or from reality, the conditions of creation and enjoyment remain the
same. Everywhere his writings demand full self-sur-
render and do not allow critical examination. To force
the spectator completely into his spell Maeterlinck
deadens the thinking faculties with narcotics and
makes the clear outlook hazy. An enigmatical, gloomy
picture at the beginning, ambiguous speeches and ges-
tures which everywhere hide a mysterious sense behind
affected simplicity, numerous pauses which seem to conceal something important and excite the hearers to fruitless worry, all this is combined and leads to a weariness

of consciousness which forms the proper basis of all suggestion.   The bodily eye closes but the eyes of the soul
remain wide open.   Reality passes away, fairyland becomes our world.

The shorter and older dramas in the complete German
edition of Maeterlinck's works are without justification
divided into two groups, ''Mystical Dramas'' and
''Every-day Dramas.''   They are all of a mystical nature in so far as in them a mysterious invisible something
approaches, making itself continuously felt, depriving
the spectator of breath and awakening in him an anxiety
which tightens his throat and makes the cold chills run
down his back.   This impression is always prominent
whether, as in *Intruse* (1898), reality is the scene of the
action, or the fairyland of fancy, as in *Die sieben Prinz-
essinnen* (1891) and *Der Tod des Tintagiles*.   '' Something peculiar must be added to everyday life so that we
shall learn to estimate it rightly,'' says Maeterlinck, and
this ''peculiar'' thing is recognized in the soul's feeling
out beyond itself into the unknown, untravelled regions.
In these ''boundless realms'' mystery dwells, horror and
fear of the impalpable encircle the traveller on all sides,
ever narrowing the circle about him and crushing in his
breast until with the despairing cry, ''I can bear it no
longer,'' he falls.

It is very comprehensible that in the quest for new and
striking impressions a genuine poet like Maeterlinck will
lose himself at times in these abysses and that kindred
natures longing for such excitement will give him grateful admiration.   But in the long run one can hardly satisfy the theatrical public with these neurological effects.
On the one hand, the morbid, on the other, the lack of
tangible material, limit the whole class in its original

form to those who are looking for mystic lyric impressions.

Maeterlinck himself returned to the basis of reality. With his theatrical cloak-and-sword play, *Monna Vanna* (1902), he gained, not without questionable expedients, a large following. This, to be sure, was his only for a time because in his next plays, *Das Wunder des heiligen Antonius* (1905) and *Schwester Beatrix* (1905), he was understood by only a few. And yet Maeterlinck exercised for some years a strong influence on dramatic writing. The conception of a domain of true poetry in which the inner life is directed outwards has taken on a new form under his influence. Those dramatists who have boxed the whole compass of possibilities for the means of expressing their poetic feelings have also halted before him but found little indeed available for their purposes.

Maeterlinck's influence is clearly recognizable in the work of RUDOLF LOTHAR. His masque, *König Harlekin* (1900), unfortunately does not devote the proper deepening of the psychical to a very effective subject, one containing in modern dramatic dress the Demetrius-theme. From this mistake Lothar's mystic dramas also suffer as *Der Wert des Lebens* (1892) and *Ritter, Tod und Teufel* (1896). In the last-named one-act drama death appears in visible form on the stage and this scene has often been repeated in these latter years. SCHMIDT-HÄSSLER has turned such a scene to good account in his effective drama *Herbst,* also the sentimental lyrist MAX MÖLLER in his *Totentanz* (1898).

The influence of Romanticism and Maeterlinck is recognizable in the use made of primitive, popular conceptions, but a new and piquant charm is sought by putting

the man with the scythe in the midst of real life among
enlightened people or his terrors are taken from him
and everything avoided which might remind one of the
skeleton.

But no one has made death appear so noble and artistic
on the stage as HUGO VON HOFFMANNSTHAL in his little
drama, *Der Tor und der Tod* (1899). Like Maeterlinck
he, too, aims in his first dramas merely at exciting feeling. But not by the aid of the peculiar and the gloomy.
In the clear light of day, exulting in beauty without
dross, his muse strides along on the heights of an aristocratic, noble humanity which is no longer touched by
the breath of the low, the wretched and the ugly. His
art shares with the Romantic the excess of musical effects, but the notes express no longer a delicate, indistinct longing; on the contrary the ear is ravished by
grand and gorgeous expressions pouring forth in swell-
ing periods while the eye delights in exquisite forms and
colors. It is a pity that this æsthetic enjoyment alone
seems to the dramatist exclusively worthy of aspiration,
because the beautiful shell lacks the kernel of strong
feeling and direct impulsive passion.

The unhappy fate of the beautiful heroine in *Die
Hochzeit der Sobeide* (1899) is intended by the dramatist to affect the soul only with light sadness instead of
overwhelming it, because the æsthetic idea of the play
has been extended far beyond the hitherto current conception. *Der Abenteurer und die Sängerin* (1899) also
aims at exciting no stronger interest than that in the
beautiful form and even then it always turns on a picture or a lyrical expression of the soul. The dramatic
form, especially in his briefest works, *Der Tod Tizians*
(1898) and *Das kleine Welttheater* (1903), is only a

means to make this note sound out full. Through the
rank climbing flowers on their high slender lattices,
which surround the artist's magic garden, one is to
suspect rather than see the outside world. The dramatic form is here resolved into a series of lyrical
poems, the speakers stand at last in no external connection whatever and all trace of a scene is lacking, let
alone an action directed to a certain goal.

To provide a definite action, Hoffmannsthal later
made use of older dramatists, as the English Otway in
Das gerettete Venedig (1905), or Sophocles in his
Elektra (1904) and in *Oedipus und die Sphinx* (1905).
The cause of this very questionable proceeding is that
the dramatist lacks real power or capacity for passionate feeling and for plastic creation. Therefore he takes
ready-made figures from his predecessors, tints them
anew with pale, modern colors, with often very unsuitable outlines of perverted, most finely differentiated
sensations or endows them, in simulation of strength
but in bad taste, with superfluous brutality. Only upon
similarly constituted spectators, without a cultivated
sense for style, can these recasts, individually charming
but on the whole worthless, have any influence. In comparison, the theatrical quality of *Monna Vanna* seems
after all the better. They signify only more or less
interesting experiments which do the stage no good and
endanger the æsthetic well-being of the public.

GERHART HAUPTMANN

In his *Monna Vanna* Maeterlinck revealed in surprising fashion a practical aptitude which, to judge from his early dramatic works, seemed to be entirely lacking in him and which had hitherto been displayed by the only one of the German "Moderns" who is recognized on all sides as the best dramatist among them, Gerhart Hauptmann.

In his work there is reflected the uncertain artistic character of the times, a continual search for a new style and new fields for subjects. Of the fifteen * dramatic works by him scarcely one will be able to hold a lasting place on the stage, but they all, the best as well as the least successful, will live on in history as monuments of this confused, uncertain and unsettled period. None of his fellow-seekers strive with such earnest zeal for the art which will offer to him, as a man living entirely in the present, the corresponding expression of his feelings. None possess in so great a degree the talent to master quickly new styles of expression and fill them with genuine intrinsic import and few have remained so free from the hurtful influences of the life and culture of large cities, of excessive sensitiveness and of decadence or have kept so well in touch with his native soil as Hauptmann.

He comes from a small Silesian town and is the offspring of poor weavers. With the impressions of his youth there was mingled the remembrance of great suffering, though he himself did not have to taste the sorrows of poverty. He saw many peasants grow rich without effort because of coal-treasures under their acres

* This number is now increased to nineteen. (L. E. H., 1908.)

and then degenerate into laziness and vice, while all around him was the prosaic acquisitiveness of the citizens of a provincial town. The youth with tender feelings and high ideals found in this world no satisfaction as landowner. He wanted to become a sculptor, but at the Breslau Art-School came to the conviction that the chisel was not to be the instrument of his development. His work was not to comprehend external phenomena but the inner nature of things and in this, according to the then prevalent faith in their omnipotence, the natural sciences were to serve him. In Jena he became Haeckel's scholar. In Berlin he looked more closely into social questions and this insight into the misery of the metropolis supplemented his earlier impressions. The despairing mood, which so often arises from the clash of youthful idealism with reality took possession of Hauptmann as well, and on an Italian journey it was condensed into his first work, the epic *Promethidenlos* (1885). Revolution does not rear its head angrily in this play as in so many "maiden" works, for according to his conviction of the legitimate nature of everything that happens, all opposition to the powers ruling in nature and society seems to him impossible and he can only show deep sympathy with the unfortunate who fall under their weight.

This conviction was still more strengthened by the influence of his brother Carl, the psychologist and physiologist with his independence of thought, and also by the circle of young authors which had collected in a suburb of Berlin and into which Hauptmann entered in 1885.

First of all the brothers Heinrich and Julius Hart

had opened the fight against senile decadence and untruth in their *Kritische Waffengänge* (1882). They desired to imbibe new life from healthy national sentiment. Karl Bleibtreu had, in his *Revolution der Literatur* (1885), tried to shatter every stone of the Bastille within whose walls all earlier authors were said to have degenerated. William Bölsche sought to find poetic form for the results of the modern natural sciences. Hauptmann came into personal and intellectual touch with them all, but above all he came under the influence of the most logical of the Naturalists, Arno Holz, and what he learned from him is shown in his first drama, *Vor Sonnenaufgang* (1889).

Its aim is to give a faithful description of certain social conditions. Exactly as the dramatist had seen them, the degenerate Silesian peasants were to appear on the stage with all that was disgusting in their disgraceful appetites, their souls completely brutalized by wealth. The most trifling characteristic was not to be wanting in the scene, and because stage-expedients were not sufficient, the author takes refuge in long descriptions in the form of stage directions. But even by this means his purpose was not to be attained. A choice had to be made from the great number of details and those received the preference, in accordance with the aggressive mood of those years, which bade stoutest defiance to the prevailing disinclination to the artistic use of what was disgusting. This tendency coincides with Hauptmann's experience. What most offends his moral and æsthetic feelings has been most deeply impressed upon him and must have seemed to him to be the most characteristic feature of the circumstances he has described. With disgust is coupled sympathy with the degenerate. From the consciousness of an inexorable fate ruling over them, there grows the conviction of a necessary connection with it; out of this develops the tragedy of their situation and with it the possibility of giving it dramatic form. In accordance with his conviction of the absolute might of the powers which settle the conditions, Hauptmann cannot, to be sure, introduce into the field against them any successful or even merely hopeful will, but he can show how the individual strives in vain to withstand them.

He places a pure girlish nature in the midst of a family circle of drunkards, adulterers and prostitutes. An ideally-minded, sympathetic socialist stretches out his hand to her in sincere love to lead her forth, but draws back because this revolt against the laws of nature must be for no good and would be avenged on the coming generation. Robbed of all hope she falls a victim.

Hauptmann wished to produce this comfortless impression and thus remain true to the demands of the school as well as to his own impressions. But contrary to his own purpose an element of joy is intermingled. Helene, this character thirsting for love, full of lofty grace and of vigorous life, may be ruined as an individual. But we cannot believe that the impulse to self-preservation in the human race, which is unconsciously revealed in her surrender to her lover, should not carry off the victory over all logical considerations. Even in the drama itself a charming love scene allows this faith to spring up. In this the dramatist shows himself mightier than the theorist, he forgets his school lesson and becomes free. The longing for happiness, for beauty, breaks out so strongly that it is inextinguishable, even if afterwards the hazy grey twilight of hopeless degeneration lies over all that follows.

Still another element is revealed in this great love-scene, the instinct for dramatic effect. Hauptmann felt that there was nothing to be gained by a description of conditions on the stage because it is a question of inner conduct, of pyschical developments brought about by conscious or still better by unconscious volition. In defiance to naturalistic dogma, he here makes two souls reveal the same strong desire, so that the spectators, like the characters themselves, forget everything else. This scene means more to the quiet spectator than all the rest of the play. In the accuracy of the characterization and in the charming sentiment of many other portions, he might also note signs that Hauptmann himself was not finding satisfaction in the artistic and scientific dogmas to which he at that time subscribed. He himself has expressed that in clear words in *Vor Sonnenaufgang*. Helene asks, "Zola and Ibsen are spoken of so much in the newspapers, are they great writers?" Loth answers, "They are not writers at all, miss, they are necessary evils. I am honorable and thirsty and desire from literature a clear, refreshing drink. I am not sick. What Zola and Ibsen offer, is medicine." But where among the spectators filled with party passion, who were present at the play in the Berlin "Free Theatre," was the ability to understand the meaning of this utterance?

Hauptmann was considered from now on an out-and-out Naturalist, whose talent and inclinations were to be at the service of the petty reproduction of external phenomena. For the sake of party prejudice, the lack of logic revealing itself in the lengthy didactic utterances of engineer Loth was overlooked and also the faults of his language, which is often by no means true to life.

In this respect his second work, *Das Friedensfest* (1890), marks a step in advance. And so also does the fact that now, instead of following the German Naturalists Holz and Schlaf and thus indirectly Zola, the novelist, Ibsen, that is, a great dramatist, became Hauptmann's model. He calls his play "a family catastrophe," but he had not yet learned from Ibsen to seize the last point of a dramatic development and so present it with its preliminary conditions that the necessity of the ending becomes clear. The new influence was still being crossed by the earlier effort to describe conditions. He, therefore, picked out from the stream of events one in which the nature of his characters and their relations to each other were significantly illustrated. Like Ibsen in his last period he does not now wish any longer to pass criticism on society but merely to present modern, morbid individuals, who are to be sure settled in their peculiarities by the condition of society.

However unsatisfactory the whole picture of this family, torn by hatred, may be, however dismal, too, the heaven that lies above them, yet there is here a far wider hope for a bright day than in *Vor Sonnenaufgang*. Significantly, at the close is placed the outlook for the victory of a firm confidence in life on the part of a womanly heart filled with love. A faint doubt disturbs the blindly accepted natural law of heredity. Surprising is the advance in technique from disjointed description to an energetic working out of characters and the collisions between them which result in a series of explosive scenes.

The action in *Einsame Menschen* (1891) once more takes a quieter course. It is a tragedy of insufficient talents, incapable of deeds. Johannes Vockerath is not a talented man and is not crushed by the might of the commonplace as would at first sight appear. That in his heart he has conquered all prejudices, has no meaning for him, because he gives way to them without opposition in order to spare his family. His intellectual significance remains an unproved assertion. He is ruined because, from fear of a decision by the stronger woman who loves him, he cannot become free. Hauptmann has here given a type of his time with convincing fidelity, a man who desires in vain to bring his over-tender feelings, which make reverent consideration his duty, into harmony with his new convictions and his striving for freedom. This suffering, in the consciousness of not being able to unite what cannot be united, is the subject of *Einsame Menschen,* the first mature work Hauptmann wrote. First, it brought cheerful recognition from outside the party to which he had up to that time been counted and awakened the belief that in him had arisen the new poet for whom the times had been looking. It was now recognized that the "drama of social conditions" could arrest one's attention as strongly from beginning to end as a plot overloaded with incidents and that it did not need the inciting expedients of what was disgusting and low. And for the sake of these excellencies one gladly overlooked the weaknesses of the too wordy outpourings of the hero and of the indistinct lines with which the most important figure, Anna Mahr, was drawn.

Hauptmann likewise showed, in the field of the cheerful, the possibility of doing away with the old developments in comedy, when his *College Crampton* (1892) appeared. It is a picture of the degenerate genius, taken from life, touching and at the same time diverting, but framed about with superfluous arabesques, all too easily thrown off.

Then he wrote *Die Weber* (1893). Earlier dramatists had never tried to sketch any but individual natures. When it had been a question of using the masses in a drama as co-acting factors, then either individual representatives would be picked out, as in Shakespeare's *Julius Cæsar* or Goethe's *Egmont,* and treated according to the principles of individual psychology, or the chorus of Greek tragedy gave the model and the feeling of unity was indicated, as in that, by some few general human impulses which are present in all. Beginnings of a "psychology of the masses" are to be discerned in Kleist's *Robert Guiskard,* in Hebbel's *Judith* and in Ludwig's *Makkabäer.* Here is already shown something of that immense strengthening force which every impulse receives because of a number feeling it in common, of those sudden transitions which arise therefrom and of the blind passion of the excited popular mind, which is swayed by quite different laws than affect the individual. But still no one before Hauptmann had attempted to make this knowledge fruitful to the drama. In Schiller's *Tell* the people spoke and acted just as every Swiss would have spoken and acted for himself. In *Die Weber,* on the other hand, the representatives of the class described there form a harp, all the strings of which begin to give out at the same time, when the air-waves strike them, low complaining or loud screaming notes, so that the individual voices together form a mighty accord, in which the peculiar quality of each is indeed discernible, but none prevails over and sounds above the other.

Die Weber is a historical drama. Free from any didactic purpose, it aims at so representing an event of the past, on the basis of a conscientious study of the facts, that the humanly significant, inwardly effective impulses stand out clearly. As the subject demands, the place of the single hero is here taken by the collective mind of the poor handweavers who start up out of dumb patient suffering with a fearful cry, become intoxicated in a half dreamy condition with good fortune and freedom and then sink back into powerless, aimless existences. In four scenes the dramatist shows us this development. With a new counterpoint technique, which one may well compare with that of Wagner, the leading motives embodied in certain figures are interwoven into a surprising wealth of combinations and at the same time the flow of the action, of the never-ending melody that carries them all, is continued. As the stage demands, one link is made fast to the next before our eyes, all joined into an unbreakable chain. The sketching of conditions here becomes, at the same time, a very valuable dramatic expedient, because volition and individuality do not settle everything, but the given circumstances and their changes are both the cause and the condition of the action. In earlier dramas by the Naturalists one could allow that the new style was a valuable technical advance; here in *Die Weber* alone has it become a necessary expression of the inherent nature of a work of art, that is, style in the higher sense.

The influence of this significant drama was both helped and hindered by the fact that its nature was mostly misunderstood. When the censor looked on it as a revolutionary drama with a purpose and therefore vetoed its performance, attention was widely called to it, and when at last its performance was allowed, it became from that point of view a drawing card, so that at first it could not be understood as the dramatist purposed. But just because of the numerous performances the author's view afterwards prevailed, viz: that *Die Weber* was only to be considered as a work of art and that its author had put nothing else into his historical material than a deep sympathy with all the unfortunate.

For the second time Hauptmann intended in the same way to conceive of an historic event in its whole course when he wrote *Florian Geyer* (1895). With the same intensive study he now worked his way into the times of the Peasants' War and set himself the mighty problem of conjuring up in its totality, out of the legal documents, this period so rent by political, religious and social factions. Every class, knight, citizen, and peasant, was to appear on the stage true to life in speech and gesture, in feeling and thought. At the same time the clash of all these opposing interests was to furnish, in the explosion of the peasant revolt, the external limits of a background that was after all scarcely to be clearly comprehended by the eye in its whole extent. Florian Geyer gave his name to the drama because the figure of the high-born leader of the peasants stands at the point where the lines cross one another. Thus in his fate there was attained at the same time a sort of dramatic recapitulation and a conclusion. Hauptmann has done really gigantic work in his artistic mastery of the mass of materials and the play represents in this respect his greatest trial of strength, in spite of the fact that there is still enough rude and unworked material left. True, the management and clear working out of the lines of direction have fared badly and, because of its length and the number of persons represented, it was shown that the drama could not be played. This alone, but not its artistic demerit, was confirmed by its complete failure on the stage. In spite of its entire want of success, this play does prove his great aim and his unusual ability to transmute the effective mass-movements beneath the surface of events and also individual deeds into dramatic scenes. With this play Hauptmann gave the first impulse to a new form of historical drama, corresponding to the modern conception of history; he set himself a high aim which was denied to the petty limitation of extreme Naturalism and struggled to get out of the confining limits of an outwardly accepted theory and be free in his creative work.

How Hauptmann worked himself free from the exclusive imitation of reality of the Naturalistic school is made clearly visible in *Hanneles Himmelfahrt* (1893). It is hardly possible to conceive of a greater contrast than that of the Silesian poorhouse and the glory-filled spaces of Heaven to which Hannele's soul mounts. We recognize in it the bold protest of the dramatist against his inclusion in the narrow everyday world. He preserves to mother earth, upon which he stands, its rights, but he wishes to let his eye wander as far as it can see. Therefore he gives in the play, first of all, a sad picture of misery and then Heaven is to light up with fairy-like colors. His angels, too, are slightly touched with the pallor of poor children and Hannele's fevered dream contains more than her childish longings can fully describe. The difficult transitions are not a success and the transfiguration at the close is decked out with too much tinsel. But these are externals which do not affect the genuine poetic content of the dream-poem and only show that a romantic and playful fancy is not Hauptmann's strong point. It is likewise to be noted even here, where for the first time the symbolical is allowed a place, that the author is not able to transmute the reflective fully and completely into dramatic scenes.

These defects of his endowment he is striving to remove because he is not satisfied with the reproduction of reality and he keeps seeking—and missing—the road to the kingdom of fairy phantasms. First, however, he returned again to his hereditary field and in *Der Biberpelz* (1893) he wrote a thieves' comedy which grouped a series of capitally drawn figures about two types of the present day. The washerwoman, "Mother Wolffen," is a masterpiece of accurate conception of a lowly soul with her shrewd impudence, her pliant loyalty and her unscrupulous use of all possible advantages. She is always pretending to be simple, and in this way comes out on top while her opponent, Superintendent Wehrhahn, inevitably falls into her nets because he wants to appear sharper than he is and is blinded by the arrogance of infallibility. The plot of *Biberpelz* is a little meagre and suffers from the repetition of the theft. To this the author was seduced by the desire to have the incident serve as a type. A sequel with the title, *Der rote Hahn* (1901), gave a

series of successful pictures of social conditions in the
Berlin suburbs, but was altogether too lacking in well-
knit composition.

Der Biberpelz, like all earlier works by Hauptmann,
could only attract that part of the public which was
ready to forego the fulfillment of the desire for an
undisturbed enjoyment of grace and beauty. In *Die
versunkene Glocke* (1895) Hauptmann composed a work
which did not demand this surrender. The subject
in this case did not entail any delineation of rude reality
nor any ugly offence against morality; still further,
the play is written in verse, is dipped in the fragrance
of the fairy-atmosphere and shows the love of a sweet,
elf-like creature for an artist with ideals. That was
the right diet for theatre-goers. Rautendelein became
their favorite character, Nickelmann amused them by
his wild appearance and his amorous quacking, and
the forest-goblin by his capers and his little, humorous
rudenesses which were gladly put up with from him.
No one worried about the obscurities in the character
of Heinrich, the bellfounder. And yet that was the
key of the play, for *Die versunkene Glocke* is a portrait
of the author, taken after the failure of *Florian Geyer.*
Hatred of and contempt for the powers of darkness,
who have plunged his difficult, artistic production into
the deep lake, the determination to make grand chimes
on the mountain, not for the present, but for a newer
and purer race of men, the fight against the ignorant
Philistines who begrudge the master his good fortune,
all this is worked into the mysterious character of
Master Heinrich and has obscured the picture. Just as
obscure is the symbolism, of which Hauptmann makes
much in this play, and the thought-content by which

he sought to give the poem greater weight. Nowhere
in Hauptmann's other dramas has one such a feeling
that this is a work with a conscious purpose which has
cost much labor.

It is given to him to succeed completely only where
he can reproduce reality with a mastery of accurate
art. Thus he created that striking and true picture of
Fuhrmann Henschel (1898). The drama seems to be
telling a story, filled out as it is with the usual accessories of explanatory and entertaining episodes. But
in reality it is a question after all of relating inner
experience. With the aid of complete mastery of all
dramatic expedients the union of a naturalistic description of conditions with a deeply moving course of
fate is carried through to completion. In Henschel,
the honest teamster with deep and tender feelings, and
Hanne, the sensual wife at his side exulting in her
strength, Hauptmann has created two very excellent
dramatic figures. For the most part, by a trick in
the arrangement of perspective, he has secured them
the leading position everywhere in the scenes out of
which, by the law of his art, they must not step. Hauptmann now aims at an illusion which corresponds in
every way to the impression of reality only that, unseen
by the spectator, he grades, by the position in the scene,
the proportion and the shading of the figures according
to their importance for the drama.

In the farcical comedy *Schluck und Jau* (1900) he
aimed at uniting joyous caprice and sadness, Shake-
sperean romantic comedy and rude realistic comic, but
the fusion did not succeed and the play is a disappoint-
ment.

It was the same with *Michael Kramer* (1900), where

the intensification had progressed to such an extent that the external incidents seemed quite indifferent. In *Der arme Heinrich* (1902) the dramatist again followed his romantic inclinations but did not make them so acceptable to the public and the critics as in *Die versunkene Glocke*. The epic material would not readily accommodate itself to the demands of the stage, and the few instances of strong external effect which the legend offered, such as the discovery of Heinrich's disease and the interrupted sacrifice, did not appear because of disinclination to all material effects. Instead the bodily sufferings of the unfortunate hero were increased to a deep soul-torture bordering on madness and to the girl was given a hazy, dawning sexual desire instead of childish inclination. The closing of the play in pomp and glory did not produce the happy effect which the dramatist had probably promised himself.

After *Elga,* which is a very superficial dramatization of a short story by Grillparzer, and was only published later (1905), he wrote a worthy companion piece to *Fuhrmann Henschel* in *Rose Bernd* (1903), a work full of great and most deeply affecting tragedy. The lot of the unhappy deserted girl, who, for fear of shame, kills her child and comes under the law, has been treated very often in literature. Goethe's Gretchen is before us as the greatest of all these unfortunates. Even though the magic, which the highest literary power alone can give, be lacking in poor Rose, after all she appeals to us as just as true, her fate just as conclusive and touching. Here, as there, we see a lovely, bright creature, whose beauty excites passion and evil desires, surrender herself unsuspectingly to the intoxicating happiness of first love until, waking from her dream, she is compelled to recognize that she is guilty, "given over to evil spirits and to a criticising unsympathetic humanity." In the deepest trouble she ripens to a woman, out of the child develops a criminal. The secondary characters also and the whole environment are conceived and reproduced just as truly and sympathetically as the heroine. The technique is admirable in its simple logic and beautiful symmetry, and assuredly a later time will count this work with its lofty and ripe art among the most valuable that Hauptmann has produced.

The highest hopes for the future of the German drama are at present centred in him. He is not the great writer who, with creative imagination, places over against the real world its counterfeit in a new self-created one, but he is reckoned among the precursors who prepare the instrument with which *the genius* may later produce the most glorious work. That he may soon appear is the wish of all who take a serious interest in our drama and who see in it not a subject of light entertainment, but the most effective means for the artistic uplifting of the whole nation.

THE PRODUCT OF THE CENTURY

THE question as to the importance to be assigned to
the nineteenth century in the history of the German
drama is not too easy to answer because a number of
very different factors are to be taken into account.

In passing judgment, the evolution of the highest
class, of tragedy, will have the greatest weight. Its
prevailing forms remained essentially unchanged during
the period. The attempts to oppose to the classic ideal
of beauty new, romantic, realistic or naturalistic forms,
have led to no generally recognized results and the
estimate of their value is conditioned by theoretical
suppositions or by the party-standpoint. The most important function in the whole range of the arts falls
to drama, that is, by the visible production of the
incidents of the sensible and psychical worlds to exercise
upon the most extensive classes of the nation an immediate, deep and æsthetic influence. For this only
Kleist and Grillparzer come into consideration along
with the great works of classic times, while for Hebbel
and Ludwig a fairly large circle of intelligent supporters is only just being formed. Hauptmann's dramas
are still too modern to allow one to judge what final
importance is to be attached to the great success of
individual works and still less can any other work
of the present be termed a lasting addition to the assets
of the past. There is, therefore, to be noted in lofty
drama neither assured progress in matters of form nor
an important increase in the number of possessions.

In contrast with this, the nineteenth century, in advancing beyond Mozart, contributed to musical drama, a work of great importance, Beethoven's *Fidelio*, and a new style, the Romantic. By two great masters, Weber and Wagner, it was carried to the highest perfection, which, it would seem, is not to be surpassed. After a long conflict the conviction is now generally accepted that Wagner's operas constitute the greatest work of the century in the whole field of drama.

The middle classes, play and comedy, the value and influence of which is determined essentially by their subjects and technique, have been lifted in two stages above the position reached by Iffland and Kotzebue. First, when "Young Germany" and its successors appropriated from the French play of intrigue the more skilful handling of plot and dialogue; secondly, when by the influence of Ibsen and Naturalism the list of subjects was extended by the moral and social problems of the present day, the characterization intensified and increased illusion effected by the aid of an analytical technique more nearly akin to reality. According to their nature and subjects these middle classes are so determined by the conditions of the times that they but rarely produce works of long life and, therefore, what is attained cannot be judged according to the number of permanent productions. The increase of average ability is, however, unmistakable when we compare the works of the best play and comedy writers of the present with those of their predecessors.

On the other hand, the rhymed tale (*Schwank*), the farce (*Posse*) and the folk-drama offer nothing but a picture of continued decay which cannot be stayed by individually better disposed writers or even those more highly gifted. The artistic requirements, which originate in dramatic form and the nature of æsthetic enjoyment, have been thrown overboard as useless ballast. Superficial entertainment by senseless comic, insipid sentimentality or even by immoral means is the only object.

To determine the total increase of new works which the nineteenth century has brought the German theatre, we now possess a reliable aid in *Der deutsche Bühnenspielplan*, which, on the basis of official information, has noted during the last six years, from Sept. 1, 1899, to Aug. 31, 1905, the number of performances in all German theatres at all worthy of mention, in 1905—427.

The dramas which have appeared since 1880 have been left unnoticed in the following list because it can not be said yet which of them will be permanent: the dramas between 1800 and 1880, however, have been collected, provided that they have been performed at least ten times in each of the last six years in all German theatres combined. If the number has been under ten, then it is a question of single experiments or of revivals set in motion by some local cause or other and one can hardly speak of a real continued existence. The figures in brackets mean the number of performances in the last six years and thus permit the varying popularity of the individual works to be seen, even if for a limited period only.

On this basis, then, of the dramas by writers whose chief work was done in the period up to 1830, the following prove to be living on the stage to-day:

SCHILLER,   *Maria Stuart* (137, 168, 157, 145, 140, 247*).

Jungfrau von Orleans (103, 85, 113, 81, 131, 185).

Die Braut von Messina (36, 44, 48, 75, 43, 131).

Wilhelm Tell (176, 131, 209, 190, 274, 412).

Demetrius (23, 35, 10, 23, 15, 74).

GOETHE,   *Faust,* Part. II (30, 36, 15, 11, 10, 19).

HEINRICH VON KLEIST,   *Der zerbrochene Krug* (37, 47, 35, 38, 53, 41).

Das Käthchen von Heilbronn (62, 49, 48, 72, 56, 64).

Der Prinz von Homburg (32, 61, 27, 32, 23, 54).

GRILLPARZER, *Die Ahnfrau* (23, 22, 26, 42, 49, 32).

Sappho (23, 37, 29, 54, 49, 52).

Medea (11, 28, 20, 52, 28, 63).

Des Meeres und der Liebe Wellen (37, 31, 40, 34, 35, 47).

Der Traum ein Leben (24, 31, 16, 15, 26, 13).

Weh' dem, der lügt (18, 13, 27, 15, 31, 30).

Die Jüdin von Toledo (22, 28, 30, 28, 36, 54).

P. A. WOLFF,*Preziosa,* music by Weber (42, 45, 43, 70, 52, 64).

Of the dramatists of "Young Germany" and their successors the following are still played:

* 1905 was the hundredth anniversary of Schiller's death.

LAUBE,   *Graf Essex* (25, 16, 13, 26, 24, 18).
             Die Karlsschüler (29, 15, 19, 16, 21, 80).

GUTZKOW,   *Uriel Acosta* (27, 24, 32, 45, 78, 38).
             Zopf und Schwert (12, 25, 18, 12, 17, 28).

FREYTAG,   *Die Journalisten* (150, 83, 93, 140,† 98,
             130).

BRACHVOGEL, *Narziss* (34, 32, 24, 23, 34, 34).

A couple of older historical dramas without artistic value are still popular because of clever technique and of popular rôles.

REDWITZ,   *Philippine Welser* (15, 17, 12, 17, 25, 17).

HERSCH,   *Die Anna-Liese* (50, 30, 43, 50, 44, 35).

Because of its regular performance in Catholic districts on All-Souls-Day the following survives:

RAUPACH,   *Der Müller und sein Kind* (16, 15, 22, 21,
             17, 22).

Otherwise this fearful dramatist and his celebrated contemporary Halm have vanished entirely. Only one work by Raimund has survived and also one by Nestroy, whose farces were formerly so very often repeated.

RAIMUND,   *Der Verschwender* (66, 70, 61, 66, 89, 98).

NESTROY,   *Lumpacivagabundus* (62, 85, 155, 91, 134,
             89).

Of the older North German farces one still survives, while the little genre picture by Schneider, *Der Kurmärker und die Pikarde,* vanished in the last year.

† 1903 was the fiftieth anniversary of the first performance.

RÄDER,   *Robert und Bertram* (95, 112, 121, 123,
                112, 116).

Undiminished attractive power for the public of
the smaller theatres is possessed by dramatized novels
with exciting complications and theatrically effective
characters.   This is proved by the stationary figures for
the plays of

FRAU   *Dorf und Stadt* (49, 58, 41, 51, 65, 62).
  BIRCH-   *Die Grille* (31, 35, 46, 38, 40, 48).
PFEIFFER,   *Die Waise aus Lowood* (42, 56, 39, 44, 32,
                48).

But the end of the older civilian comedy is coming,
for only its chief representative has reached the limit
of ten performances in each of the last six years.

BENEDIX,   *Die zärtlichen Verwandten* (24, 46, 49, 55,
                53, 100).

For the present the writer who may be called his
next of kin keeps his position better:

L'ARRONGE,   *Mein Leopold* (36, 60, 66, 59, 68, 83).
               Hasemanns Töchter (62, 76, 66, 70, 82,
                131).
               Doktor Klaus (107, 97, 90, 169, 119, 133).

The plays which Moser wrote, partly alone, partly in
collaboration with others, serve for the lightest entertainment with continued success.

GUSTAV   *Das Stiftungsfest* (48, 25, 28, 41, 15, 30).
  VON MOSER,   *Ultimo* (28, 16, 18, 25, 17, 15).
               Der Veilchenfresser (54, 79, 95, 75, 114,
                83).
               Der Bibliothekar (48, 47, 41, 53, 98, 58).

Moser and   *Der Registrator auf Reisen* (21, 38, 34, 35,
L'Arronge,   22, 57).

Moser and   *Krieg im Frieden* (77, 75, 65, 58, 123,
F. von   146).
Schönthan,

If we ask what has been preserved of those writers
who, as representatives of Realism, were looking for
new paths, away from the beaten highway of old art
and of routine, the result as it refers to Hebbel, the
greatest German dramatist of the century, is really
shameful, for he can appear in our list with only one
work:

Hebbel,   *Maria Magdalena* (21, 33, 47, 27, 39, 43).

while *Die Nibelungen,* which comes next to this tragedy
in number of performances, really ought not to be
cited because in the last four years it has not reached
the limit set:

Hebbel,   *Die Nibelungen,* Parts I and II (16, 8, 11,
            30, 22, 26).
            Part III (13, 4, 10, 20, 12, 6).

So little does Hebbel's mighty creation find a place
to-day on the stage. Fortunately the signs are increasing that the theatre and the public are beginning
to show him greater consideration and it cannot fail
that for his works there is coming a time of more fre-
quent performance.

Otto Ludwig, too, has not a full claim to be mentioned with the one work which is to be considered
here, for the number of performances of *Die Makkabäer*
amount only to 4, 12, 2, 1, 3, 2.

LUDWIG,   *Der Erbförster* (7, 43, 31, 40, 32, 18).

There is at least a continued interest shown in this
affecting drama, because the goodly numbers are not
due to local success but are scattered over a compara-
tively large number of theatres.

A striking confirmation of what was said of Anzengruber is found in the fact that the popularity of his
four works which are still given repeatedly stands in a
reverse relation to their artistic merit:

ANZEN-   *Der Pfarrer von Kirchfeld* (84, 71, 78,
  GRUBER,   123, 162, 114).
              Der Meineidbauer (71, 45, 51, 37, 60, 41).
              Der G'wissenswurm (13, 26, 15, 34, 32, 61).
              Das vierte Gebot (23, 37, 39, 23, 28, 36).

In the field of opera the following older works are
to be mentioned on the same hypothesis as the spoken
drama:

BEETHOVEN,   *Fidelio* (165, 145, 154, 167, 176, 182).

WEBER,   *Der Freischütz* (240, 278, 243, 234, 248,
                  261).
              Oberon (56, 97, 56, 34, 79, 47).

MARSCHNER,   *Hans Heiling* (48, 41, 54, 37, 33, 34).

KREUTZER,   *Das Nachtlager in Granada* (87, 73, 60,
                  77, 54, 75).

LORTZING,   *Zar und Zimmermann* (167, 154, 190, 165,
                  198, 201).
              Der Wildschütz (105, 76, 95, 97, 96, 62).
              Der Waffenschmied (164, 145, 155, 139,
                  158, 179).
              Undine (186, 192, 217, 150, 184, 185).

Flotow,   *Alessandro Stradella* (76, 57, 58, 50, 55, 67).

Martha (167, 182, 190, 173, 180, 187).

Nicolai,   *Die lustigen Weiber von Windsor* (147, 137, 143, 141, 137, 154).

Later, because of the overpowering influence of Wagner, only two other German operas in the old style acquired a lasting influence:

Brüll,   *Das goldene Kreuz* (28, 28, 40, 34, 33, 25).

Goldmark,   *Die Königin von Saba* (32, 43, 31, 49, 25, 47).

Otherwise the victory belonged to the great tone-dramas by the "master," the number of performances being of all the greater importance because the most of them abound in insuperable difficulties for the smaller theatres:

Wagner,   *Rienzi* (43, 30, 33, 21, 35, 42).

Der fliegende Holländer (202, 155, 194, 187, 188, 218).

Tannhäuser (269, 273, 269, 283, 286, 326).

Lohengrin (294, 294, 297, 284, 311, 341).

Tristan und Isolde (53, 72, 59, 60, 87, 68).

Die Meistersinger von Nürnberg (142, 171, 138, 176, 191, 192).

Das Rheingold (52, 77, 105, 82, 80, 96).

Die Walküre (128, 131, 162, 148, 147, 168).

Siegfried (64, 86, 89, 115, 113, 127).

Götterdämmerung (59, 76, 78, 97, 85, 80).

Apart from some operettas, the quoting of which can be spared, all dramatic works from 1800–1880 have been named, which the German theatre may to-day consider as its possession. The number appears large in comparison with the dramatic inheritance which earlier centuries left their heirs, but it is to be noted that the nineteenth century passed without great changes in regard to the prevailing tendency of art. So soon as these take place then doubtless almost all that belongs to the passing vogue in art will sink into oblivion. The experience of earlier times teaches that only a few works of superior and absolute merit or of lofty contents in general human significance defy the changes of time. Therefore one may now prophesy even for the greater number of the above-named dramas a sure death. This fate will overtake first the older middle-class plays and comedies, standing, as they do, on a lower plane in psychology and technique.

If the sum total of the century in this field were decided only by the compass and merit of the increase in new works, then a halt might be made right here. But two other factors demand notice also in the history of the drama, dramatic art and the public.

At the beginning of the nineteenth century the German drama possessed scarcely a single worthy temple. The spectators assembled in wretched, uncomfortable, dimly lighted theatres, the stage offered for illusion a very meagre aid with its badly painted movable scenes and views and very rarely was care bestowed on historical fidelity in scenery and dress. The staff was small in number, the actors had to play the most varied rôles and everywhere had to assist in opera as well, which only here and there had a few trained singers at its disposal. The regular theatres had to pay their own way, only a few courts supplied a small grant. Of course the expenses were not very high because of the simplicity of the external apparatus and the small pay of the actors. The latter were glad if they got a sure home and had a modest income.

To-day all the large and medium-sized cities in Germany possess respectable, often indeed, grand theatres. They have now at their disposal a complicated machinery and artistically painted decorations of deceptive accuracy; also a very great number of objects for equipment and costly costumes, true to history. However great this progress appears, it brings this disadvantage in its train, that quick changes within an act are impossible because of the large apparatus to be set in motion every time. This breaks the conception, especially in the older plays, divides the acts into a series of separate scenes and thus destroys the sense of the dramatic technique of the drama. The most modern dramatists have sought to suit themselves to the given circumstances by avoiding any change within an act and, wherever possible, having the whole action proceed in the same space, a procedure favored by the modern technique which brings only the last stage of the action on the boards.

The enlargement of stage-space, undertaken for the sake of the opera, is prejudicial to combined play, while the extensive audience-chambers of more modern theatres deprive the players of contact with the public and force them to overstep naturalness in speech and movement, in order that word and gesture may be understood by all hearers. A remedy for this grave drawback is to be desired, especially for the large towns which are able to build special smaller theatres for the play, because the chief tendency of dramatic art is now toward an increased refinement of psychical expression and suggestive effects.

As the performances of the players live on only in the subjective impressions created by them, a comparison of former ability with that of to-day is in general excluded. Even the testimony of the same witnesses in the field is not to be trusted, because first impressions are strongest and youth is far more easily moved to enthusiasm than circumspect age. Objectively it can only be said that the present actors have as a rule command over a higher intellectual culture than their predecessors, and that specialization of rôles must increase the possibility of having full command over special departments. From this it may be concluded that the ability to act well must, in general, have increased, but the great increase in theatres and the numerous staff which they employ has brought it about that the demand for really talented and satisfactorily trained actors can not even approximately be supplied. Therefore the complaint is general and justifiable that there is scarcely a theatre in condition to offer a completely satisfactory cast for a great drama.

Decisive progress means, by contrast, the driving out of empty rhetoric and of "stars," a more careful development of combined play and an endeavor to produce more direct effect by finer description of motives, and by a staging which is sympathetic, historically true and corresponds to actual life. To the conductor is now granted the proper and necessary power of regulating, according to his wish, the combinations of work on the part of the numerous forces in front of and behind the scenes, so as to help the play to become a unit in embodying the purposes of the writer.

The expensive external apparatus, the increase of the number of the staff and their salaries, which reach excessive figures through competition for the services of every available actor, have greatly increased the expenditure of the theatres. Because of this, regard for income has become far more compulsory than before, even for Court theatres. In spite of the subsidies granted them, they are, after all, even more than formerly, dependent upon the ticket-money, as the grant in all cases covers but a portion of the expenses.

Thus there is impressed on all theatres more sharply than ever the character of an industrial institute, and in few places does success attend the effort to keep out what is artistically distasteful by a sensible balancing of material and ideal interests or to withstand the debasing inclinations of the great masses.

Only those theatres which are conducted with this noble purpose are to be recognized, without reservation, as homes of art and valuable factors in the spiritual life of a nation. They alone can exercise an undisturbed, strong and ennobling influence on the public. And yet, with the yielding to the need for entertainment, which is practised by the great majority of theatres, a higher tendency is not excluded, and along with silly farces and low operettas is often found in the same place, a successful effort to offer meritorious works in dignified form, a compromise which is necessitated by the double mission of the stage of to-day.

The demand that the lighter wares, rhymed tale (*Schwank*), farce (*Posse*) and operetta, be completely banished can probably never be fulfilled. An alto-

gether too large proportion of the public demands chiefly
this pabulum and the only thing to do is to endeavor
to arrange the relation of the artistically valuable to
the worthless as favorably as at all possible. The complaint that the public of to-day takes less pleasure
in the good than the public of the past is refuted
by an impartial test of the facts. At no time have the
works of the classic writers of more modern and most
modern times enjoyed such eager appreciation as at
present. Under Goethe's managership of the Weimar
theatre two to three evenings in a year on the average
were given to the plays of Shakespeare, which may
well be considered a reliable standard, a number now
often increased tenfold. That a trained dog or the
actor of an ape's part should come on the stage of
one of the best theatres in plays written expressly for
them, as happened seventy years ago, seems now excluded.

In this respect public taste has surely risen and if
now senseless drollery and reckoning on concupiscence
appear in more disgusting and artful fashion than before, it must after all be conceded, that apart from
some theatres in large towns, no further decadence is
to be noted in this respect during the last period, while
on the other hand interest in the higher classes of drama
seems to be increasing. On this very important point
one's judgment can, of course, not pretend to any
general validity, when supported by observations made
in a number of places, because local conditions are too
varied. The contending, contrasting forces are a rigid
and narrow conception of art and society and coarse
materialism on the one side, and a newly awakened
striving for beauty, intensification and deepening of

thought and motive on the other. They hide the present, their scene of battle, in opaque clouds of dust, especially in the field of that art which, more than any other, is conditioned as to time for those who create and those who enjoy. But the struggle itself, the eager party divisions are after all a sign that living interest is on the increase. In this the first preliminary condition of intelligent enjoyment and of a turning away from a mere sense-enjoyment is fulfilled in a rather high degree.

The historian is a prophet looking backwards. His sole business is to interpret the signs of the past. Particularly in the history of art, all prophesying as to the future is excluded. Only this can be said, that the nineteenth century, after long neglect, has again begun to prepare the ground for an art of lofty style, and therefore its last effort for the drama has not been without influence. Whether it will bear fruit, whether a new crop will spring up out of the newly ploughed furrows, depends on those who will cultivate this field in the future and win new harvests with the aid of the creative warmth of the sun of genius.

INDEX

1. AUTHORS

219

2. WORKS.